THE CUSTOMER LOYALTY PLAYBOOK

12 Game Strategies to Drive Improved Results in your Business

JERI QUINN

Nell,
may all your
business dreams
come true
Jeri Quinn

Special discounts and customized versions on bulk quantities of Driving Improved Results books are available to corporations, professional associations, and other organizations. For details contact Driving Improved Results, 610 5th Avenue, #833, New York, NY 10185 Email the author at jeri@DrivingImprovedResults.com

First Edition
ISBN: 0989943208
ISBN-13: 9780989943208

Advance Praise For
The Customer Loyalty Playbook, 12 Game Strategies to Drive Improved Results in Your Business

Engaging, stimulating and full of wonderful surprises, *The Customer Loyalty Playbook* is just like Jeri Quinn herself -- an invaluable resource offering great insight and exercises that lead to growth and fulfillment. I'm excited about using Jeri's great new book to find new ways to better serve my clients and to boost my income. Thanks, Jeri!
Tom Martin, President, Tom Martin Media, LLC

Great step-by-step methodology for customer loyalty. Each chapter gives specific steps you can utilize immediately.
Linda Stinson, President, RLS Focused Solutions

Now you don't need a library to help you build great customer loyalty! In this one book you have everything you need to turbocharge your business. A loyal customer base is the foundation of a strong business, and this playbook shows you step-by-step how to build the business you've dreamed of. I just wish Jeri had written it sooner!
Norman Usher, Founder, Winterhill Consulting Ltd, UK

One of the fastest ways to grow your business is to develop loyal customers that will buy more and refer you to their friends. In this book Jeri gives you the key simple steps you can take to create more raving fan customers and dedicated employees, who are committed to the success of the company.
Joy Putnam, Peak Performance Coach

Jeri's book is more than a book about customer loyalty; it's a book about leadership. If you implement the strategies and "playbook ideas" Jeri has defined, you'll not only gain incredible customer loyalty, you'll become a great organization.

Mike Goldman, President, Performance Breakthrough

There are many books that touch upon the issues Jeri addresses in *The Customer Loyalty Playbook*. But this one is special because it aggregates difficult concepts into one cohesive, easy-to-grasp narrative for small business owners. The case studies are especially helpful. A must read.

Bruce Stout, President, Rainmakers Forum

Who knew there was a connection between our vacations and our business customers? The Playbook makes logical and useful connections between our work and how it impacts customers, and allows you to create your own spiderweb of connections that will open your eyes to how you can build a next-generation business for yourself and your organization. Great insights and an easy read.

Robyn Rickenbach, President, Springboard International Inc

Any business owner, including myself, will benefit from this book, getting a lot of new ideas about how to improve every day operations. It answered so many questions that lingered in my mind. So much knowledge from such short reading time. I've always believed that my success depends on a good team of people (it's impossible to make it alone) and loyal clients that are happy and comfortable to stay with me for all their insurance needs. This book has motivated me to organize my thoughts and implement all the ideas I've had in my mind for some time. I feel it puts me on the right path to succeed with my business. Thank you again.

Daniella Kirfeld, President, Interwest United Insurance Brokerage Inc

The Customer Loyalty Playbook makes sense and is specifically designed for small and medium companies to make an immediate difference in the bottom line. Need a topic for a sales meeting? It's here. Setting goals for the next quarter? Use this. Rallying renewals? Jeri has your back. The basic blocking and tackling guide for small and medium sized companies puts ready to use and easily executed plans at your fingertips.

Carey Davis, Business Broker, Transworld Business Advisors of NY

This is a book that every entrepreneur and their team needs to read. Without keeping your existing customers happy and developing new customers, a company cannot not grow and prosper. Jeri has written a playbook and road map that is easy to understand and will yield immediate results in growth and profitability.

Larry Putterman, Serial Entrepreneur, Business Coach, and founder of LarryPutterman.com

Loyalty is earned….it stems from actions that are taken and the words that are spoken by employees. The author of this book takes you through a set of straightforward management practices that will inspire your workforce and improve your bottom line. Whether you are a business owner, manager of people or a consultant practitioner, you will be able to apply what the writer conveys by way of examples, easy to understand diagrams or the provocative questions and references she offers that, if applied, will certainly help to improve performance and bottom line results.

Norm Gauthier, Managing Partner, Heritage Hill Partners Inc

Jeri's ideas and concepts are easy to comprehend and more importantly, easy to implement. Following her recommendations will lead to increased profits for any type of business.

Neil Miller, Founder, N.L. Miller Accounting

DEDICATION

To my parents:
Phyllis Reeve who instilled in me a love of learning and the aspiration
to become an author.
Chester Reeve who inspired and modeled the balance of an easy going
nature with a persistent work ethic.

To my husband Richard Quinn
For all the love and support to grow in my own way

To my children
Tara, Brendan and Shane who teach me more every day about how to
live life more fully

ACKNOWLEDGMENTS

I express my deepest gratitude to the many people with whom I've worked to produce the tools and ideas presented in *The Customer Loyalty Playbook*. Thanks goes to the moral support provided by the members of BNI chapter 25 in New York City, especially Tom Martin (publicist), Siho Ellsmore (who created the cover and interior graphics), Christy Goldfeder (sales copy), Angela Matthews (social media strategist). Having these individuals as part of my team allowed me to expand the capability and reach of this book and its impact on the world. All the BNI chapter 25 members have been interested and supportive which has empowered me to finish the book. They've also helped promote the book and referred me to speak about the book.

A special thanks goes to June Clark (editor) who revealed my blind spots about what was missing and confusing. June's experience, encouragement, dedication and thought provoking questions helped me consider what I was writing from the reader's point of view.

Members of two professional mastermind groups provided caring intelligent comradeship, accountability and many suggestions. Thank you to Robyn Rickenbach, Norman Gauthier, Kevin Collins, Kevin Brimhall, Hank Sullivan, Mike Goldman, Linda Stinson, Eric Merz, Norman Usher and Denise Corcoran. Your words of encouragement and accountability deadlines helped me get moving again when I was stressed and blocked.

I acknowledge Joy Putnam and Grace Cheng for constantly challenging me and giving me tools for overcoming inertia and overwhelm.

Their caring stand for me and this book has kept me on track to bring this project to completion.

This book would not have been possible without the support of my closest friends, Barbara Block, Jeanne Friedrichs, Evelyn Kalinosky, and Mike Andrews whose faith in me to live into my potential and share my knowledge and experience kept me moving forward.

Doug and Polly White, Rick Lochner and Greg Stuart, fellow consultants/coaches, have inspired and challenged me with the publication of their own books. They've provided words of wisdom, examples, insights gleaned from their own mistakes, and gems of knowledge around the promotional use of their books. Thank you for sharing your wisdom with me.

Special appreciation goes to Dick Quinn, my husband, for the continued support and interest in this project. Thank you for being my biggest fan.

The material in this book was honed over the course of my career by using it with clients. Their continual feedback of what works and doesn't work has allowed me to have insights into what is useful and what communicates effectively. Through the leaders I've coached, the groups I've facilitated, the entrepreneurship classes I've taught, these concepts and tools have become more clarified, more useful, and easier to implement. I salute all the people I've coached, facilitated, taught, and consulted with. You are the true heroes of this book. I have grown in your listening of me. I give you my heartfelt appreciation.

CONTENTS

THE FOCUS OF THIS BOOK

Did you know that a 5% increase in customer loyalty could add an extra 25-100% of profit to your bottom line?

Did you know that it costs 5-8 times more to get a new client than to keep an existing client?

Did you know that loyal customers who buy regularly help you have predictable cash flow?

This book gives you the 'why' and the 'how' of customer loyalty so you can have these benefits in your business.

INTRODUCTION

"In the NFL, the playbook is a sacred hardbound diary of trust. It's an accumulation of decades' worth of knowledge, tweaked and perfected, sectioned off by scribbles and colored tabs."

--Elizabeth Merrill, ESPN.com

This book has been written for the owners and executives of small and midsize businesses. Over the last thirty years, I've worked to make the companies I've owned successful. I've also consulted with and coached small and medium-sized business owners, helping them create bottom line results and quality lifestyles.

Government statistics state that 50% of small businesses fail in the first 5 years. If you've got a new business, I'm sure you don't want your business to be part of that statistic. If your business has been running for over 5 years, you may want to keep your business moving in a positive and lucrative direction. The intent of this book is to support you in creating sustainable successful results by focusing on key elements.

As a small business owner, I know what it's like when the cash flow is tight. With no big corporation to guarantee my salary, "I ate what I killed." My companies learned to do more with less. As small and medium-size businesses, we deal with tighter budgets for hiring and outsourcing. We sometimes have family members or friends working in the business, which introduces complex dynamics and succession issues. On the other hand, we can get closer to our customers and be more responsive to their needs. We care more about our employees because we know them personally. We are free to create a vision for our business and ourselves. Most of all, we do what we love and love what we do.

So why did you start your business in the first place? It's important to take stock of your reasons to be in business so you can maintain your motivation and empower yourself.

Through working with thousands of business owners, I've learned that these are the main reasons why people want to own their own businesses:

- To make money with no upper limit
- To have the freedom to create a flexible schedule
- To be your own boss, do what you love and have control over your own work (and do the job or run the business better than the last boss you worked for)
- To bring a great idea to life
- To build something successful and derive pride, recognition, fulfillment
- To provide jobs for family or community
- To give yourself a job because you can't find a job working for someone else

Most small/midsize businesses are inextricably tied to their owners' personal lives. That's the nature of the beast. You want your business to serve your life, providing a livelihood and a quality of life that you desire. What good is a great business if you lose your health or your family or your friends or your personal values/standards? What good is making a lot of money if you aren't proud of the way you acquired it? And what if you're not enjoying your work? Your business is meant to enhance your life, not diminish it.

The Customer Loyalty Playbook will help you design structures in your business so that you can achieve your quality of life goals around time, money, relationships, and accomplishments. The focus of these structures is to improve customer loyalty, which is the backbone of a highly effective business. I know my life worked better when my company's leadership was customer-focused; when knowledgeable, committed employees took ownership of their work and delighted the clients; when effective marketing systems were attracting our ideal clients; and when we generated profits from our clients' loyalty.

You may get so caught up in the day-to-day whirlwind of getting things done that you may overlook seeing the big picture of where you are going or what you can do proactively to take your business to the next level. You may even lose sight of the reasons why you started your business in the first place.

This book's underlying purpose is to help you focus on the big picture, readdress your goals, and create a solid infrastructure proactively and in spite of the whirlwind. It will also show you why improving your relationships with employees, clients, and customers is key to your success, and how to more effectively attract, manage, and retain these relationships.

There are a lot of books on the market that address these issues. What's different about this book? This is an easy to read, image-based playbook. Just like a football playbook it defines game winning strategies. A football playbook presents formations, runs, passes, and movement on the field. It shows the plays in diagram format and then gives detailed descriptions. This book does the same. It identifies the playmakers, presents formations of people in the right positions, guides the coaches and players, gives step by step tactics, and sets up measurements to put on the scoreboard. A winning game plan creates momentum that builds on itself to create a victory. And that's what *The Customer Loyalty Playbook* can do for you and your business.

According to research collected by HubSpot, 90% of the information transmitted to the brain is visual and visuals are processed 60,000 times faster in the brain than text. Any sports coach will tell you the same thing.

My own work confirms HubSpot's research and the sports coach's instincts. In my work coaching and consulting with small and mid-size business owners and their teams, I've found that images have been instrumental in comprehending concepts quickly and easily. Over the years, I've developed a collection of pictures, matrixes, and diagrams that I've used in my work--my own playbook that I've shared with clients. I will now share this material with you as a way to help you understand business growth strategies more intuitively.

Each chapter in the book presents an image that illustrates a crucial business concept that you can include in your own team's playbook. There is an explanation of why this concept is of benefit and how to incorporate it in your business. This is followed by a case study that shows successful use of the concept. Discussion questions are included to help you further explore the concept and stimulate discussion with your team. Supportive information, including full-color versions of the images for reproduction, is available at www. CustomerLoyaltyPlaybook.com.

Some people believe knowledge is power. But I believe that *applied* knowledge is power. It doesn't matter how many great business books you read, the knowledge is worth nothing if you don't apply what you've read.

That's what makes this book different. It is actionable by its very definition as a playbook. Each image conveys a concept visually, creating more immediate understanding. The chapters are short. The questions facilitate execution in your own environment. Each chapter is complete in itself and can be used separately from the other chapters in any order you wish.

Here is one way to use this playbook. Select an image from a chapter you want your team to understand, download it from the website, print and distribute, or project it on a screen for your whole team to see. Have a few members of your staff pre-read the chapter's explanation and case study to summarize for the rest of the team. Then, let them proceed to ask the questions suggested in the book. Engage your staff in contributing their ideas. Select the best idea--or a combination of ideas--to implement that moves the company forward. You've started to practice distributed leadership, which generates your staff's active interest in implementation. You're now already practicing one of the things the book suggests. Each chapter can be used at a "lunch-and-learn" or team meeting to build employee involvement in making the business more customer-centric.

I invite you to visit my websites www.customerloyaltyplaybook. com or www.drivingimprovedresults.com to share how you've used this book to create more success in your business.

CHAPTER 1
THE WHY AND HOW OF BUILDING CUSTOMER LOYALTY

Did you know that a 5% increase in customer loyalty could add an extra 25-100% of profit to your bottom line?

Did you know that it costs 5-8 times more to get a new client than to keep an existing client?

Did you know that loyal customers who buy regularly help you have predictable cash flow?

Customer loyalty, customer service, and *customer experience* are terms that have been bandied about a lot recently. You can apply them like a bandage to an organization through talk and add-on programs. But a bandage is only a short-term remedy. Sustainable effectiveness is only achieved when the infrastructure of the business is customer-centric.

The focus of this playbook is to help you—the small or mid-market business owner—see, in a clear and simple way, the importance of *why* you need customer loyalty and *how* to build it. Using pictures, we will discuss how you can enhance your infrastructure so that customer loyalty is a natural outcome.

But before we get to the pictures that show *how,* let's talk about *why. Why* do you want to improve the loyalty of your customers? *Why* is customer loyalty the backbone of your business? Why do you want to play this game?

Here are nine compelling reasons *why*:

1. **Loyal customers generate profit.**

   Let's look at a customer from the business owner's profit-making point of view. When a customer makes a purchase, you subtract all the direct costs of providing the product or service. What's left is called *gross margin*.

   If the customer buys once, this gross margin covers the customer acquisition costs--all the costs associated with attracting and pursuing that client, such as your company's branding, marketing, and sales efforts. Many companies don't know their true customer acquisition costs because they have never tallied all of the costs associated with attracting customers: sales commissions, marketing, advertising, website and SEO, social media, business cards and brochures, trade shows, marketing salaries, promotional items, and portions of management salaries used to put all these elements in place. If you add up all of these expenses and divide the total by the number of new customers obtained during that period, you'll get a more realistic sense of just how much up front cost you've invested in each one.

   You probably will not make a profit from a customer until he purchases a second or perhaps a third time. Since you're paying a substantial cost to land that customer, the more he buys, the more you leverage your investment in the acquisition of that customer.

   If all you get are first time, single purchase customers, you are probably losing money on each one of them unless you're charging a high fee. It's only when customers make repeat purchases (three or more in most cases) that they truly contribute to your profitability.

2. **Loyal customers buy more.**

   From the customer's point of view, the first purchase is a test to see if buying from you works out well and makes him happy. It doesn't matter if it's a product or a service—your organization is providing something and you've made a commitment to him. He wants to see if you're reliable, hassle free, and can keep your promise. The second time he patronizes your business, he's looking to make sure the first time wasn't a fluke—he wants confirmation that this buying experience is repeatable and trustworthy. The third time, he actually becomes a customer because he knows that his needs will be met and that it will be a pleasant and positive experience. He now trusts you and may be ripe to purchase more from you and at a higher price point. You now have the opportunity to *cross-sell* and *up-sell* because your customer is comfortable enough to try new things you recommend. You are now a trusted vendor. He is giving you more of the dollars that otherwise might have gone to a competitor.

3. **Loyal customers give referrals.**

Customers who are delighted with your product or service can't wait to spread the word to colleagues or friends. They are excited and may even show the product or the results of the service to others around them. An ideal client is bound to have other friends or colleagues who can also become ideal customers or clients. Word of mouth is the least expensive and most cost-effective customer acquisition strategy. It can also be the most powerful because the relationships that the customer has with the people he refers foster an added level of trust for your business.

This is especially true today. People share their best and worst experiences on Facebook, Twitter, Pinterest, Yelp, YouTube, and other social media networks or blogs—not just in writing, but also with photos and videos. Consumer websites compare products and buying experiences. Loyal customers are now more likely than ever to express their positive or negative testimonials online. This organic and unsolicited word-of-mouth referral from a loyal customer is worth its weight in gold.

4. **Loyal clients are not as price sensitive.**
   Loyal customers are not only looking at the purchase price. They expect and want a delightful and meaningful buying experience. They are willing to pay extra for your company's product or service to get the personal recognition and individualized experience they desire.

5. **Loyal customers help your business thrive by paying on time, which provides you with cash flow.**
   Your faithful customers love what you offer, buy regularly, and pay when expected. This establishes a steady, predictable cash flow from which you can pay your expenses and subsequently reinvest in more manpower, training and development, customer service software, and other business enhancements.

6. **Loyal customers interacting with an engaged staff generate an upward value spiral.**
   Loyal customers become loyal because your staff provides delightful experiences and extraordinary value. In turn, dedicated customers improve your employees' morale, enthusiasm, and commitment, enhancing the customer experience even more. This impact is positive for business in many ways. Employees have more pride in their work and in job satisfaction. Long time clients develop personal relationships with specific staff members and that leads to a stronger, more enduring business relationship. There is also an increase in personal fulfillment. Employees stay longer reducing the expense of recruiting, rehiring, and retraining. They become more productive and efficient. Satisfied employees also attract more ideal clients. This "virtuous circle" leads to the next reason to work at customer loyalty . . .

7. **Loyal customers give your company competitive advantage.**

   The virtuous circle creates enhanced profits and cash flow, giving your company a financial advantage. You then have the resources to enhance your product/service and customer experience even more. This continuous improvement results in your company taking market share away from your competitors. You can then become more selective in your choice of customers.

8. **Loyal customers lead to reduced servicing costs.**

   Every time you acquire a new customer, you set them up in your order entry system, your delivery system, your e-mailing list, and your customer survey system. The more often you service that client, the more you know about their preferred delivery arrangements, payment plan, and order specifics. You've also trained them on how to reach you and who to ask for, which improves communication and response time. Your staff gets more efficient at servicing that customer and anticipating her needs.

9. **Loyal customers are more forgiving.**

   Even when striving to provide a quality experience, mistakes can happen. When they do, loyal clients will accept your apology and the "fix," and move on. They look at your company from the point of view of caring and trust, so that imperfections have less significance. In fact, the speed and quality of your fix creates a "wow" factor that reinforces how good your company is. This creates more positive stories for testimonials and referrals.

Building customer loyalty multiplies sales revenues and reduces costs. It generates cash flow and sustains growth. It creates an energetic, motivated and fulfilling workplace. But what does it do for you, the owner of the business? These are the ultimate reasons why you personally want to incorporate customer loyalty as the core of your business.

FOUR PERSONAL ADVANTAGES FOR BUILDING A CUSTOMER LOYALTY FOCUSED COMPANY

1. You'll have a better quality of life where you can leave work at a reasonable hour, delegate tasks with confidence, and even take a lengthy vacation. You get to enjoy your family and friends.
2. If you want to sell your business, it will have more value as a self-sustaining organization, rather than one that needs you to do all the work of the business or land all the clients. A self-sustaining business is more attractive to an investor and will likely command a higher price.
3. Pride of accomplishment for growing a successful enterprise.
4. More money in your pocket. The more profit you make, the higher your salary and bonuses.

AND NOW FOR THE HOW

Now that you understand the reasons *why* you should build an organization focused on customer loyalty, *how* do you do it?

You focus on the customer more than you ever thought was possible.

This process doesn't happen overnight; it evolves just as the company culture evolves. It takes time to build infrastructure and start the ball rolling, just like it takes time to develop a winning sports team. However, once it gets started and becomes part of your company's culture, it's highly sustainable.

The chapters that follow focus on *how* to build and sustain customer loyalty. By continually maximizing and optimizing these strategies, your reputation will grow and your business will thrive.

These are the four main areas of focus:

CREATING CUSTOMER LOYALTY BY ENHANCING YOUR LEADERSHIP

Hockey legend Wayne Gretsky said, "I skate to where the puck is going to be." As a leader you will want to know where your business is going and how to get it there. If you aren't developing yourself as a next level leader now, you won't have the skills or perspectives to get you or your business there tomorrow.

A leader is always educating and developing himself. That includes reading/listening to business books, articles, and magazines. It also means getting to know yourself, your talents, and abilities. Leadership is a people-centric capability. If you are more task-focused, you need to sharpen your emotional intelligence. It may mean learning how not to react with anger or negativity, or how not to overwhelm your staff. It means learning how to bring the best out in others through listening, coaching, getting their buy-in, and taking a stand for them when they don't necessarily believe in themselves.

Practice is required in being a good leader, whether creating an effective team from a group of unrelated individuals or understanding the effect of your communications and the impact of your decisions. You can read books and attend lectures about these topics but to really master these skills, you must take what you learn and do it. Small/midsize business owners especially are known for learning by being in action, taking risks, learning through experience, making mistakes, and failing forward. Action happens on the field, not in the stands.

How is a *customer-centric* business different than a *company-centric* business? What does a culture of distributed leadership look like as compared to a culture of centralized leadership? A leader needs an open mind to explore concepts, use creativity, and then know when to hone in on the best option and make a decision.

Leaders who want customer-centric businesses with highly engaged employees and loyal customers intentionally build businesses with infrastructures that support those expectations. This empowering infrastructure is not a department that gets added on or something that the account manager owns. It's not a "Buy ten, get one free" loyalty program either. This customer-centric empowering infrastructure is built into every nook, cranny, job description, incentive plan, performance review, customer relationship management technology tool, transaction evaluation, customer recognition program, recruiting/hiring procedure, on-boarding and training program, development and leadership process, marketing promise, brand experience, the facility décor, and the language staff uses. It's an integral part of the business plan. It's the business' *culture*.

Business thinkers use the term "healthy organization" to refer to a company where the culture is welcoming, the employees are fully engaged, where they have habits and attitudes that support the focus on the customer experience, where they are happy, growing, and their personal and professional goals are being fulfilled.

As the business owner, you are in charge of your culture. That's one of your main jobs. Many owners of smaller businesses aren't aware of this and that holds them back. This takes skill and an awareness that you need to develop before your business will grow reliably and be scalable. Winning teams have coaches that purposefully provide the edge needed to face tough competition. You can become that coach.

Your managers play a critical role in your company's culture. In many growing businesses, the managers are long-term employees who received promotions as others got hired below them, but have never been trained as managers. Surveys show that the top reason most people leave a job is because of the ineffectiveness of their manager. Managers act as liaisons between the executive team and the individual contributors. Their roles in a growing organization fulfills a very necessary function—one they must prepare for if they are going to supervise those on the front line with your customers.

Chapters 2, 3, and 4 present game strategies that focus on enhancing your leadership to earn customer loyalty.

CREATING CUSTOMER LOYALTY BY ENGAGING YOUR EMPLOYEES

Many of us have seen employees that are 9-to-5-ers. They put in their time and collect a paycheck. They are not invested in the company's success. They don't care much about the quality of their work. If they deal with customers, they might not care if each customer has a great experience.

On the other hand there are organizations where employees are engaged in delighting customers and finding ways to make things happen as customer advocates. They take initiative to make sure the customer experience is better than expected. They care about the quality of their work, the contributions they are making, and the success of the company. They look for ways to cut costs and make projects run more efficiently. They want to learn. They make many of their own decisions. They care. They are a team.

How do you grow an employee culture like that?

1. You set up an environment of coaching and collaboration rather than command and control.
2. You hire those who are most likely to flourish in a well-led environment and weed out those that sabotage your efforts.

Leaders who empower and develop their employees earn trust and commitment. Leaders who inspire their employees with a clearly stated vision create clarity, which results in everyone working toward the same end game. Successful leaders encourage employees to "own" their jobs, contribute their own talents, and make and learn from their mistakes. Leaders who care treat their employees as unique individuals, giving them plenty of acknowledgement and respect in every situation.

How does all this contribute to customer loyalty? The way you treat your employees is they way they will ultimately treat your customers. Your employees are the face of your business. By their words, actions, attitudes, and commitment to success, they define your brand and the perception in the mind of each customer. They are also the guts of your business. They do all the work. They define the quality. They keep the promises. They meet the deadlines. They provide what the customer is buying. When the customer returns and eventually becomes loyal, it's due to the positive actions of your staff.

Part of your role as a leader is to make sure all your employees are doing work that suits their talents, competencies, and preferences. Are they playing the field position for which they are best suited? Is each one of them in the right role and giving the best they have to give? If so, you will get the best return on investment for the salary you're paying.

Are they being developed so they can have career paths? At different levels of the organization different skills are needed. Are you setting each person up for success by providing the help they need for maximum success? If you were the owner of a sports team, wouldn't you be investing in maximizing each player's performance?

Each person has thoughts, reaction patterns, habits, and mindsets that are part of his character and comfort zone. To really delight each customer, we can't just say on a bad day, "I'm not in a good mood today. I'll delight the customer tomorrow." In a customer-centric culture, your employees must learn how to shift their mental state when necessary and put the customer first.

Chapters 5, 6, and 7 present game strategies that focus on engaging your employees to earn customer loyalty.

CREATING CUSTOMER LOYALTY BY ENGINEERING THE CUSTOMER EXPERIENCE

When you are a customer, how do you like to be treated? Personably? Warmly? Are you pleased when a salesperson remembers your name or what you ordered last time? Does the employee's positive attitude come through? Do you feel that the salesperson cared? Do you feel supported and special? Do you feel better after the interaction than before?

The Sales Executive Council conducted a study of the purchase of 20,000 different products. They asked consumers about the criteria that most influenced their buying decision. Here are the results:

19% - the company's reputation, brand and website
19% - the product itself and the company's ability to deliver
9% - the value to price ratio, analysis if the item was worth the money
53% - the sales experience

When creating the infrastructure to earn the client's loyalty, we generally put our attention on all the processes that go into developing the first three items—the 47%. It would be advantageous to place emphasis on the other 53%--the sales experience.

You have a lot to gain by providing a great sales experience to your customers. What if every time your customer purchased something from your organization, the experience was so easy and delightful that it felt like a vacation? What does it take to create that experience and build that bond?

There are points of connection during interactions with your customers where they are practically begging you to connect with them, say something special, offer them some fun and laughter, show them you care, and truly listen and engage. You can leverage these points to provide a much richer customer experience. You can train your staff to consistently deliver this type of rewarding experience with customers and to anticipate the customer needs and desires. The keyword here is *anticipate*. Customers love to have their needs anticipated. It makes them feel recognized and understood without having to ask to be recognized and understood. Don't leave the design of the customer's experience to chance—engineer all those points so the experience is consistently delightful.

Chapters 8, 9, and 10 present game strategies that focus on engineering your customers' experience to earn their loyalty.

CREATING CUSTOMER LOYALTY BY FOCUSING YOUR MARKETING

The purpose of marketing is to grow more business and attract more customers or clients. But do we want just any customers or clients? No, we want *ideal* customers and clients, the ones who will get the most value from our products and services, who are fun to work with, who pay promptly, and refer us to others. Some prospects are not a good fit and are unlikely to become loyal. So, to this extent, loyalty is dependent on us targeting the right prospects.

The first rule of marketing is to know whom your company is targeting. Is it businesses or consumers? Who are your buyers and what are their issues? Having a clearly defined target market is key to zeroing in on specific needs and wants. When buyers see themselves in the picture you paint of your ideal clients, they become attracted to you like moths to a flame. Providing them with solutions tailored to address those needs and desires is the natural next step. When the fit between the people you attract and the service/product you offer is perfect, you have opened the door for a client to become very loyal. It's a necessary first step. The second step, getting them to step over the threshold, is determined by your customer experience.

What is your growth strategy? You can grow by expanding the number of products/services you offer. You can also grow by targeting additional markets. Another alternative is to create a customer experience that outshines your competitors. As your business' customer loyalty increases over time, your reputation and profits will also increase, often growing your market share. Focusing on the customer experience now is a marketing strategy that sets the foundation for the development of new products/services or expanding to a new geography in the future.

How will your sales revenues be generated? What mix of products and services and target markets will determine your company's income? You can and should plan this each time you do annual planning. Build loyalty into these interactions, too. There are opportunities to up-sell and cross-sell based on the trust you and your team have built with your clients. You've earned this trust; now leverage it.

Potential customers and clients expect that the quality of your marketing efforts reflect the quality that they will eventually experience should they invest in your product or service. Regardless of your budget, make sure that your marketing activities provide a quality experience. Good marketing builds on itself. One activity builds on the awareness generated on the previous activity, especially if they are linked.

A push into any of these three growth areas requires first-rate communication. It's similar to an offensive campaign in sports. Using your playbook is the best way to teach a complex offense.

Chapters 11, 12 and 13 present game strategies that focus on your marketing to enhance customer loyalty.

AGAIN A REMINDER . . .

It is not necessary to read the chapters of this playbook in sequence. Each concept presented is executable on its own and each one you implement will build on the one before so that you will see actionable results for yourself, your employees, and your customers.

Happy implementing!

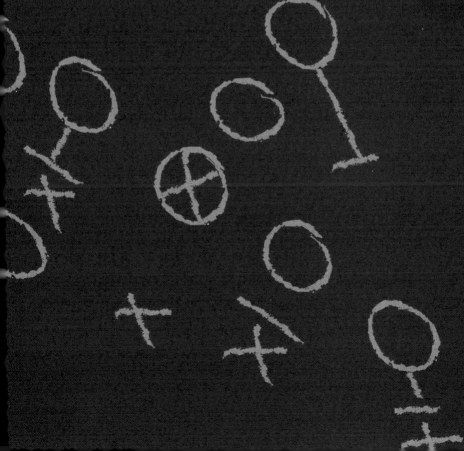

LEADERSHIP

CHAPTER 2
THE CUSTOMER/CLIENT-CENTRIC BUSINESS

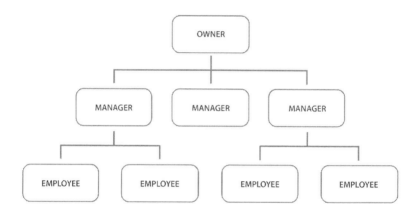

Does this look familiar to you? It's an organizational chart with the CEO at the top, the managers under him, and the staff under the managers. It looks like a triangle with the point at the top.

This business has a top down management structure. The leadership is centralized. Decision-making occurs at the top of the hierarchy.

Did you notice that there is no customer in the picture? This business is focused on the business of having an organization. Its structure is not customer-centric. While some people in the organization may be attentive to customers, the structure of the business is set up to be more focused on the business than on the customers being served.

The people at the bottom of this structure are often customer service people or support people. They are likely to have the most contact with the customers. How they interact and connect with the client will determine if the client feels unique, special, and attended to.

In spite of their important roles, members of the customer service staff generally have the least decision making power, the least training, the least pay, and the least influence on the rest of the organization. This is ironic because they have the ear of the customer and the whole organization relies on the money they generate. That money gets generated because the customer service and support service people have created strong relationships with customers and clients. Yet that importance is not reflected in how they are hired, empowered, supported, paid, or trained.

It's worth noting again: *The customer is not in this picture.* If you want customer loyalty—which has been shown to make businesses more profitable and sustainable—the customer should be the *focus* of the picture and the people who interact with that customer need decision-making ability and a great deal more respect and support.

Inserted with permission
Copyrighted by Resource Associates Corporation

What if we turned the triangle upside down? What if we put loyal customers at the top? Each interaction with a customer service rep or a support person is actually where all the work of the company comes into focus and gets translated into a purchase. It's a moment of truth. After all our work developing a product or service, building our business model, and developing our organization, does the customer buy what we offer? This is the point where the rubber meets the road. Does the customer have a delightful experience or just a satisfactory one?

In this reverse model, management and executives support the customer service staff in making great customer experiences happen. The managers support the staff and the CEO supports the managers.   This is the distributed leadership model that many forward thinking and nimble companies are adopting because it drives profits, drives customer loyalty, and drives employee retention. A key component of internal customer satisfaction is creating a culture of engagement and empowerment.

Your employees will treat the customers the same way management treats them. If management genuinely cares for each employee as an individual, motivates and trains them, empowers, trusts and encourages them to try new things, make mistakes and grow from those mistakes without retribution, then the internal customers—your staff—will feel validated, self-confident, and sure of their skills. This will come across to your external customers. The decision-making ability will create velocity and the possibility of "wow" experiences that will delight customers and result in customer loyalty.

On the other hand, micromanagement, lack of professional skill training, lack of personal development, the absence of supportive coaching, no decision-making capability, and a lot of top down authoritative management will create a culture of non-engagement and 9-to-5-put-in-my-time attitudes. This leads to a culture of apathy, mediocrity, not caring about quality, and lack of loyalty from the staff. Needless to say, when these unmotivated employees interact with clients, those same attitudes are communicated and there is no impetus to generate customer loyalty.

As the leader and playmaker, you get to choose the model and create the company culture. You can choose not to care about culture and just take what comes, which usually leads to indifference and lack of initiative on the part of your employees and customer/clients . . . or you can proactively create an internal culture that leads to increased sales, greater employee retention, better customer relationships, and the profitability that results from customer loyalty.

As a leader, whom do you have to become to create an empowering client-centric profit-generating culture? Successful leaders have developed themselves in the areas of emotional intelligence, authenticity, coaching, compassion, listening, asking good questions, facilitating great meetings, inspiring others, goal setting/achieving and accountability. They look for ideas and models on the Internet. in print publications and from successful people. They actively seek personal development and ideas on how to create and nurture a loyalty generating culture in their companies. Great coaches in sports and business are always growing their soft skills because they know that's what provides the winning edge. Winning coaches live their personal integrity because everyone is looking at them as the model.

The diagram above shows three components: People, Systems, and Strategy. In any business these interact under the guidance of the leadership model just discussed to create internal customer satisfaction. *Strategy* determines how the business will act in the world. *Systems* are necessary to standardize processes so they become efficient and cost-effective. *People* make everything happen—they contribute their energy, motivation, and time to accomplish the strategy, build the systems, and connect to the clients.

So the people—and the culture generated from their combined energy—make the strategy and the systems work or not work.

Appropriate in this instance are the words usually attributed to management consultant Peter Drucker: "Culture eats strategy for lunch."

CASE STUDY

A food packaging and distribution company understood the concept that customer service people were the key to growing their business and to the loyalty of their customers. Their customers were food retailers that would place regular orders. The company realized that they were going to face increased competition from foreign competitors and, if they didn't up their game, they stood to lose a lot. They had always put customer service last, providing no training, no management, few online tools, a manual ordering process, and no service standards. Employees who no longer fit in other roles were moved to customer service. The salespeople wanted nothing to do with them. They were simply considered order takers.

As a result of our work together, the executives formed an in-house task team comprised of individuals from multiple departments and led by the CFO. They hired an experienced customer service manager who reported directly to one of the company owners. They developed a database of their products and an order entry system that a customer service person could use when talking to a retailer. This order entry system not only gave product details, but also recommended related products that the customer might like to try.

The company developed a training program and instituted job descriptions and criteria for joining their team. They sensitized the customer service staff to the benefits of connecting with clients with empathy. They looked at their highest selling customer service representative and studied her habits. She generally spent more time on the phone with each client and got to know each one on a more personal level. The result of this deeper relationship was that clients were willing to trust her recommendations about new products, ordering quantities, and product life cycles. The company then encouraged the other customer service representatives to adopt the habits of their successful colleague.

The culture of the team changed. They each felt valued and important. Other people in the company started requesting to join the customer service team. Most importantly, sales increased 10% in just a few months, especially in the areas of up-selling and cross-selling. Over time, the culture of the customer service team began spreading to other departments.

PLAYBOOK IDEAS: HOW CAN YOU APPLY THIS TO YOUR ORGANIZATION?

1. Are your customer service representatives recruited and hired with care so that they proactively create the face and brand of your company?
2. Are your customer service and support representatives paid well? Trained well? Respected and listened to?
3. Do you have feedback loops so that information obtained by the customer service staff (through being in direct contact with customers) influences future decisions at all levels of the company?
4. Do the company executives have regular meetings with the customer service/support representatives so the executives can continuously learn more about their customers?
5. Do the managers and executives see themselves as supporters of the customer care team and provide them with training, support, tools, coaching, etc?

6. Does your company use customer relationship management (CRM) tools and software to track customers, their phone conversations and email, their order history, and documents exchanged (e.g., quotes, contracts)? Do your customer service/support people have access to these tools so they can enter data about last conversations, customer birthdays/anniversaries, the names of their children/pets/spouses, the places they go on vacation, their hobbies and accomplishments, health issues, and so on?

7. Examine where internal customer satisfaction is demonstrated and where it isn't. Discuss the impact this has on relationships with customers.

8. On a scale of 1 to 10 (with 10 being highest), how would you rank your organization as a customer-centric company as modeled in the inverted triangle with customers at the top?

9. What could your company do to improve that score? What easy action could the company take right now that would have the most positive impact?

Additional supportive material and opportunities for growth can be found at www.customerloyaltyplaybook.com

CHAPTER 3
KASHBOX AND THE HEALTHY
ORGANIZATION

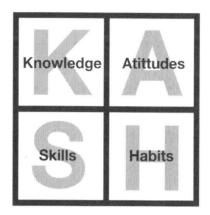

Inserted with permission
David Herdlinger, Herdlinger Associates

Noted business coach, David Herdlinger, developed the concept of the *Kashbox*, which is illustrated in this diagram.

When hiring and retaining employees, most businesses focus on and invest in **k**nowledge and **s**kills (the K and S boxes on the left) whether offering training sessions on site or through industry associations for continuing education credits.

However, many business owners fail to realize that when an employee doesn't work out, the reasons are usually due to performance issues, which are symptomatic of **a**ttitudes and **h**abits (the A and H boxes on the right). Without proper and positive attitudes and habits, people are less likely to succeed in their jobs, regardless of the knowledge and skills they possess. An employee who exhibits all four qualities will turn KASH into CASH for your company.

Ask any sports coach. It's usually not the players' skills that are seriously deficient. It's the attitude, work ethic and habits of excellence that the player embodies that turn him into a champion.

What factors impact attitudes and habits? These include, but are not limited to:

- A strong work ethic
- The motivation to do a quality job
- A commitment to achieve and grow
- Time management
- Interpersonal communication
- A positive desire to engage and contribute

LACK OF EXECUTION IS PROPORTIONAL TO THE GAP BETWEEN THE LEFT AND RIGHT SIDES OF THE KASHBOX.

When there is a gap between an employee's attitudes and habits and his skills and knowledge, he can say or even demonstrate on a test that he knows a lot but he doesn't commit to applying it on the job. He may have a list of what to do but procrastinates and can't organize his time. He often does a job with poor quality even though he knows what good quality looks like. He has skills but has a hard time contributing them in a team environment where he has to interact with others. He gets something 95% done and then abandons it.

Having all the knowledge and skills in a particular job or industry will not make a person a better contributor to his organization if he's not motivated to work consistently throughout the day, can't communicate with team members, or can't manage time. A player can know the plays while in the locker room, but if he can't execute on the field when it counts, what good is his knowledge?

There are a few business owners that claim they hire for attitudes and habits, and that they can teach the skills and knowledge once the new employee is on the job. But, in my experience, most business owners and job descriptions are focused on knowledge and skills because these qualifications are easier to specify and detect. A few attitudinal or habitual elements may be noted, but are usually not emphasized during the hiring process or training.

CREATING HEALTHY AND SUSTAINABLE ORGANIZATIONS

How do you narrow that gap between K&S and A&H? This is where the concept of the *healthy organization* has been developed. A healthy organization is one in which there is execution and performance—but that is only half the story. The other half addresses the employees as people—living, breathing, caring, and emotional individuals with lives, families, goals, aspirations, and energy to manage. Your employees are not robots working to meet performance goals; they are people who want to be seen and valued as unique, special, and worthy of individual respect and recognition. They want to have fun, be inspired, feel needed, get excited, and be valued as contributors. Valuing people this way gives them the impetus and self worth needed to increase productivity. When people feel valued, they naturally give more of their time and energy.

In order to create a healthy organization, leadership needs to pay attention to culture. Within an empathetic and empowering culture, performance goals are easily executed and exceeded, and business growth is sustainable over a long term.

There are two things you can do to narrow the gap between the left and right sides of the Kashbox and to create a healthy and sustainable organization that executes and achieves its goals. First, you can make sure everyone you hire is properly vetted for their attitudes and habits as much, if not more than, their skills and knowledge. This involves using assessments for a more objective hiring process. Second, you should train and develop each individual to maximize his personal and professional potential.

HIRING ASSESSMENTS

It is difficult to assess attitudes and habits through an interview alone. That's why larger companies often use assessments to get clearer pictures of potential hires. Smaller companies often forgo the assessments to save money. However, every mis-hire is extremely costly—up to three times an annual salary when all is said and done. Assessments help to identify if a prospective employee is a good fit culturally and has the decision-making and communication habits that will make him a valuable player. The point is to hire someone who can be a long term "A-Player." Assessments can help you understand what these people look like so you can hire more of them, regardless of how well they interview. Assessments can also help you pinpoint personalities that balance teams. Once you choose to hire someone, the assessment report tells you what kind of training the new person will respond best to so he can be brought up to speed quickly.

DEVELOPING EACH INDIVIDUAL

Here's a formula that points out how K&S (knowledge and skills) interacts with A&H (attitudes and habits). It is results driven and creates changes in individuals that produce long-term results. It also creates great succession planning and low turnover.

A company is made up of individuals. To create a cohesive empowering culture, it takes working with each of the individuals.

$$\frac{A\,(T+S+K)}{v+b} + 3PG = BC \rightarrow SIR$$

Inserted with permission
Doug Brown, Paradigm Associates

Let's go through this formula backwards. The SIR stands for *sustained improved results*. We all want improved results, both professionally and personally. And we want these results to be sustained over a long term, not just a short-term boost.

Did you ever hear the quote "insanity is doing the same thing, over and over, and expecting different results"? It makes sense that in order to get the improved results, you need a behavior change. BC stands for *behavior change*.

You walk around in a comfort bubble that contains all the behaviors that are easy, habitual, natural, and convenient for you to do. In order to expand your comfort zone bubble to include a behavior change, you must set an intention to do something different. That becomes a *goal* (G). In fact, you may have several types of goals: *people, profit,* and *planet* (3P). In this case, the formula so far has you developing goals in the areas of relating to people, maximizing profit, and utilizing sustainable environmental resources so that you can get out of your comfort zone and create behavior changes that will drive sustained improved results.

So where do these goals come from? T stands for *talents* that we all have, our unique abilities that we do well. S&K, as you know, stand for learned skills and knowledge. You've learned and practiced many different skills and have absorbed lots of knowledge. For instance, one skill you have is how to use the Internet. But do you use it to procrastinate or to be productive? You also know how to speak. Does that mean you aren't anxious when you have to speak in front of hundreds of people?

The determining piece that will create the goals leading to change is the A. It's the multiplier of the whole formula. *A* stands for *attitudes*, habits of thought and the mental recordings that play in our minds. Attitudes vary from person to person. You can have a positive or negative attitude, an open or closed attitude, a narrow or expansive attitude, confident or self-doubting attitude, a scarcity or abundant attitude, and so on. Some of us are more conservative in the risks we take; others are adventurous and love to take on new challenges. These underlying attitudes sometimes sabotage our ability to be productive, grow, improve our businesses, act like leaders, have big visions, recognize opportunities, or handle change. But how are these attitudes formed?

If we go below the line in the formula, we see v+b—*values and belief.* Our value and belief systems were imprinted on our unconscious minds, as we were growing up, by our families, teachers, friends, cultural heritage, and previous work experiences. Researchers say that 88% of our daily actions are done on autopilot. Did you ever get in your car to drive from point A to point B while thinking about something else, so that when you arrive you don't even remember driving there? It's like the car drove itself.

In terms of the formula above, the development experience asks each individual:

- To become aware of those value and belief systems (v+b) and to choose to change the ones that no longer serve us, so that attitudes (A) can be conducive to growth, fulfilment and expansion
- To learn more about our unique talents (T) so that they can be fully utilized and maximized in appropriate job roles and development of potential
- To fill in any gaps in business skills and knowledge (S&K)
- To develop goals (3PG)
- To create behavior change (BC) through practice, application and feedback
- To obtain sustainable improved results (SIR) that are astounding and long lasting

A	(T+	S+	K)	+	3PG	=	BC	→	SIR
Self-Belief	Unique Abilities	Metrics & Systems	Cash Management		Goal Setting		Behavior changes		Profit
Confidence		Sales & Marketing	Industry Knowledge		Time/Work/Life Balance		Accomplish Plan		Vacations
Bigger Thinking		Innovation	Customer Loyalty		Business Planning				Asset Value
Empowerment		Coaching Skills	Employee Engagement						
Values Orientation		Emotional Intelligence	Communication						
Positive Expectancy		Priorities Alignment	Accountability						

LEADERSHIP OF THE HEALTHY ORGANIZATION

You can apply the above formula to the business environment. Drilling down to exact attitudes, talents, skills, knowledge, goals, behavior changes and improved results look like this. Offering assessment, training and development to employees can cover these areas.

Specifically, as people are individually taken through a development process and they explore their talents, skills, and knowledge (in the T, S, and K columns above), items in the A column come up and are dealt with within the context of what is important to each individual. There is a focus on setting goals (3PG column) and accomplishing them (BC). The ultimate rewards (SIR) are a natural outgrowth of the development work. Because this development work is in depth, specific to the person, and addresses personal growth, it leads to long-term change.

Individual development work changes the health and the productivity of the organization, which in turn, produces a return on investment. Nothing helps a team more than increasing the motivation and skills of each individual player.

Bandages and quick fixes don't produce a return on investment. Good leadership is a habit–so is not-so-good leadership—which is why change requires time, practice, application, feedback, trying again, and having "aha" moments to change those old autopilot habits. Just like athletes practice over and over again, leaders build their leadership muscle by getting plenty of practice.

CASE STUDY

Scott, a Vice President of a large insurance company, runs a department that sells policies to small and midsize companies and also processes the paperwork for the insurance carrier. He has a staff of about six people.

Wayne, an employee at the insurance company, has been working there for 20 years. He's a relationship guy and that was fine when there were few regulations and minimal paperwork involved in each transaction. Wayne likes people and is easy to talk to. But as much as he is talented in this area, his ability is insufficient in today's world. Even when he talks with and sells to clients, he still needs to get paperwork filled out correctly, get signatures, give quotes out knowledgeably, and take full responsibility for getting whatever help he needs. Wayne was failing in his job. He was letting lots of details slide by and not bringing them to the attention of colleagues who could help him or provide the necessary support. And he was leaving at 5:00 p.m. each evening without making sure the job got done.

What was he lacking? He lacked a work ethic, communication skills, attention to detail, a sense of responsibility, caring about the ultimate outcome for the client as well as the company, motivation to do a quality job, commitment, and time management. He assumed he knew his job and he certainly understood part of it. But the attitudes and habits necessary for success were clearly missing—this is a classic example of lack of execution and a big gap between the left and right sides of the Kashbox. Wayne was at serious risk of losing his job.

Scott got approval from the CEO to work with Wayne for 30 days to see if he could turn him around. He coached Wayne by asking him about his goals and dreams, what he thought was missing in his attitude and behavior toward his job, about what he would do if he lost his job, and, if his job was at risk, what he was willing to do to keep his job. Based on those answers, Scott created a list of tasks and procedures that he shared with Wayne, letting him know that if he mastered these tasks and applied himself for 30 days, he could keep his job. Wayne would also have to seek training from the others on the team and report to Scott daily and weekly about what he accomplished.

Wayne then stepped up to the plate and successfully saved his job. The company, in turn, retained and enhanced the capabilities of its long-term employee.

The hero of this story is really Scott. Scott had the vision to see that Wayne had value to the company, even though he hadn't yet developed many of the attitudes and habits that could put that value into action. Through coaching, Scott empowered Wayne with penetrating questions that gave Wayne the option—and full responsibility—for staying or going. Scott's proactive leadership allowed Wayne to make difficult choices and commit to the outcome he wanted. Often, changes in attitude and habit come about when there is a functional or emotional breakdown. At that point, the individual has to choose and live by his choice. Scott runs a healthy department since he addresses the needs of his staff so that they can become engaged, committed, and masterful at work they find meaningful. Wayne's turnaround happened within a culture of six other people who helped train and encourage him.

PLAYBOOK IDEAS: HOW CAN YOU APPLY THIS TO YOUR ORGANIZATION?

1. Does your organization execute well? What is missing on the right side of the box (attitudes and habits) that may be preventing execution?
2. Do you have a healthy organization? Describe how you would rank your company on a scale of 1 to 10, low to high, in terms of:

   - Empowering culture
   - Dedication to doing excellent work and going above and beyond

- Providing employees with opportunities to develop personally (vision, values, goals, choices, life plan)
- Providing employees with opportunities to develop professionally (seeing the match between their personal vision, values, goals, choices, and life plan and the company's vision, values, goals, and strategies)
- Devising written career development plans for each person
- Ensuring that each person knows his unique talents and is in a position to use them in her work
- Providing all candidates being considered for employment with personal assessment tools to measure attitudes and habits, as well as conducting multiple interviews and reference checking. (This is in addition to whatever is needed to ascertain skills and knowledge.)
- Ensuring that every employee is recognized and treated as a unique and special individual with a life, a family, and personal goals and aspirations

3. Are your managers trained to coach and collaborate? Or are they using command and control tactics to manage? Have the managers been through a process of personal and professional development? Have they been trained to expand their emotional intelligence?

4. Does your staff get things done? Are people held accountable for what they say they will accomplish? Are tasks completed on time and on budget?

Additional supportive material and opportunities for growth can be found at www.customerloyaltyplaybook.com

PEAKING FOR SUCCESS

STRATEGIC ORGANIZATIONAL DEVELOPMENT PROCESS

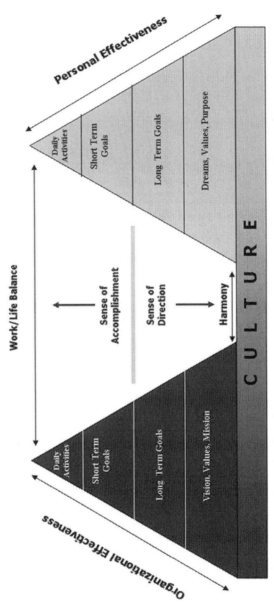

CHAPTER 4
DUAL PYRAMIDS

How can we maximize the return on investment made by any business owner in having employees and paying salaries? The keys to answering that question are discussed below and are expressed in the diagram above.

If we look at the two pyramids, we see that that one represents the *company* and its visions, values, mission, long and short-term goals, and actions. The other represents the dreams, values, purpose, long and short-term goals, and actions of the *individual*. The degree to which the left pyramid and the right pyramid are in alignment with each other is the degree to which each individual is a naturally committed and motivated employee.

How would you like to have a company filled with naturally committed and motivated employees?

What are the key attributes found in well-run companies with naturally committed and motivated employees?

THE LEFT PYRAMID

In a well-run company there is a clear overall *vision*. The executive team has clearly communicated that vision over and over in company meetings. The vision is the company's north star. It's their "I have a dream" statement. Great executives don't just sit in an ivory tower or a corner office--they manage while walking around the company. They talk to their employees, reinforcing and acknowledging behaviors in line with the vision. They share stories about the company's employees and clients that exemplify the vision and give it life. The company's mission is a five-year goal that aligns with the company's vision.

There are clearly delineated *values* that guide the corporate culture and can be seen in everyone's behavior. Here are some examples:

From Zappos
- Deliver "wow" through service
- Embrace and drive change
- Create fun and a little weirdness
- Be adventurous, creative, and open-minded

From 3M
- Innovation; "Thou shall not kill a new product idea"
- Absolute integrity
- Respect for individual initiative and personal growth

Walt Disney
- No cynicism allowed
- Fanatical attention to consistency and detail
- Continuous progress via creativity, dreams, and imagination
- Fanatical control and preservation of Disney's "magic" image
- "To bring happiness to millions" and to celebrate, nurture, and promulgate "wholesome American values"

These values are often defined on the company's website and may include stories that illustrate how the values have been put into action. Even if a company doesn't have written values (and many small companies don't), everyone knows them, because they are practiced. If a company does have written values to guide behavior, the big question is: *Are the practiced values and the written values the same?"*

The defined company values should be communicated to every employee and demonstrated by those at the top. If they are, then company leaders are trusted and respected. If not, then it doesn't matter what slogans appears on wall charts and wallet cards. Nobody really believes in the bogus values. When there are clearly delineated values that are conveyed well and practiced, employees often blog about them, acknowledge each other for showcasing them in their work, and tell clients about them. Guided by these values, company employees can go above and beyond to satisfy and delight clients or customers.

The company has **long-term goals**, often called **strategic initiatives** or **1-5 year goals.** The company also has **short-term goals**, which are those that everyone is working toward in the next few months. These goals comprise the company's operational business plan. Your team works toward the company's vision by implementing strategic initiatives (that represent long-term goals), which cascade through the levels of the company as short-term goals. These short-term goals define the specific **actions** each department and its staff must take. When these actions are taken, the longer-term goals are achieved.

This is the structure that incorporates and aligns all four levels of strategy and execution. It is important to clearly communicate the company's vision, mission, and goals to your staff so they can achieve them as a group. That's the left pyramid.

THE RIGHT PYRAMID

Each person lives by a set of **values**—principles and standards of behaviors that are either instilled by family and community or gained through life experience. These values define and guide behavior. If employees' values align with the company's values, they will feel comfortable in the company and, ultimately, more effective and productive.

A person who has taken the time to examine all aspects of his life is much more aware of his values and the possible discrepancies between what he says and what he does. He may choose to redefine his behavior by his personal standards of what's right and wrong. Even if the employee has not participated in a formal self-examination process (often called a developmental process), if his values match the company values, he will feel right at home. However, if he has no problem taking office supplies for personal use and his company frowns on that, there is a misalignment of values and he may not be a good fit. This may be a bigger issue than office supplies if clients are funneled off to an employee's side business, or cash is collected that doesn't hit the books, or an employee refuses to do a certain job when the company policy is to help with everything (often required in a small business setting).

Each person has **dreams**. These may include getting an education, getting married, or having a family. Or these dreams may be to rise to a high level in a particular industry, start a business, become a homeowner, travel extensively, create a nest egg for retirement, or create a non-profit. If an employee sees that her dreams for herself are aligned with the company's vision, she will be motivated and committed to work toward a mutually beneficial outcome. If she sees herself building skills, contacts, and leadership experiences that she can use to grow her overall career while moving the company toward its overall vision, she will be more invested in contributing her energy, passion, and time.

Do you know your life's **purpose**? Have you thought about it? Have you written it down and journaled about it? People who have discovered what they are dedicating their lives to act with focus, determination, and commitment. They become known as leaders because they take a stand. If your employees know their life purposes and those life purposes are in alignment with the company's vision and mission, then each employee's personal commitment and dedication becomes what they share with the company.

A person who has been through a formal developmental (self examination) process has given a lot of thought to what she wants for herself long-term. She has explored her own life's purpose and meaning. Her written purpose puts her on a path to create the kind of life that leads to what she wants rather than to merely tolerate what might come her way. It is a much more fulfilling life.

She has created **long-term goals** that reflect her overall dreams and has a desire to turn them into reality. She has chosen a career path that contributes to those long-term goals and when the company culture supports her, she is motivated to give her all.

She is also aware of the **short-term goals** that will lead to the achievement of her long-term goals. She has created the steps needed to reach each one and takes the necessary **actions** to achieve them.

In an ideal circumstance, employee goals are aligned with the company's goals and a common set of values that everyone embraces. There is alignment vertically from top to bottom inside each pyramid as well as horizontally between the company and the individual's values, vision/dream, mission/purpose, short and long-term goals, and actions. In reality, however, it rarely works in this ideal manner. The company may not be clear on its values or its vision. Even if it is, these values and visions may not be well communicated and reinforced regularly. They may only be communicated to upper management or they may fail to exist altogether.

Employees at all levels in a company may not know their individual purpose. They may have a sense of what's important to them and possess values they learned in the past. But they have not written them out and clearly identified or evaluated them. They just know, innately, what does and doesn't feel right or comfortable. Younger employees, in particular, often know their short-term goals but are not knowledgeable about or committed to long-term goals, since they are discovering life as it "happens."

Despite lack of awareness or misalignment within the company pyramid or within the individual pyramid and miscommunication between pyramids, a company is still responsible for results and results are generated by a committed workforce comprised of employees who are not only knowledgeable and committed to personal standards and goals, but also committed to achieving and improving the company's objectives. How can the risks of lack of awareness and misalignment be mitigated so the company's vision can be achieved?

THE ROLE OF THE MANAGER

The key person to foster employee commitment and productivity is the manager or team leader. This person translates the company's vision, mission, values, and short and long-term goals to those who report to him. The manager also helps each employee see how his own dreams, purpose, values, and goals fit within the framework established by the company. The manager is the go-between between upper management and the individuals in his department. The manager acts as a coach and identifies alignment (or misalignment) between the employee and the company.

The manager asks the big questions: *How will the skills you learn help you in your career? What do you want to accomplish personally and how can we align that with what we are working toward as a department? How can your special skills and talents be best utilized for the company's long and short-term goals? Are you learning skills and attitudes that are useful outside of work, such as teamwork, communication and customer service?* He arranges for training and development so employees can be more self-aware and improve alignment of their own dreams, purpose, values, goals and actions so they can bring more dedication to the job. He cares about his employees. As a result, they care about their work, their colleagues, and their clients.

The manager also communicates the department's ideas and concerns to the executive team. He advocates for his employees' best interests and conveys their feedback about customers and what is or isn't working to the executives in order to help them in their decision-making. Because the manager is in the middle, he is a liaison who helps create and improve alignment of value, vision, mission, and goals within the whole organization. The manager is also key in helping those above and below him improve communication.

WHO BENEFITS? THE CUSTOMER.

When employees and all levels of management are clear and committed to the same vision, mission, values, short-term and long-term goals, their actions are working in unison. The culture then has focus and continuously moves in the same direction, as opposed to a stagnant culture that just swirls around a cloudy center. The difference is palpable.

How can you improve alignment among everyone in your company? It's a five-step playbook strategy that happens over time.

1. The executives must determine the company's vision, mission, values, and short-term and long-term goals. These should be written down and discussed with employees often. In fact, it's even better when the employees help to generate them.
2. Have all employees at every level participate in personal and professional development so they achieve clarity on their personal dreams, purpose, values, and goals. This will help their actions align with their goals. So often what we say and what we do are not the same, and they should be in order to be effective in life and on the job.

3. Ensure that managers understand their "sandwich" roles. They can practice/role play the kinds of questions, communications, and coaching that will involve and engage individual employees in the alignment model. This way, they become empowered to speak up and share with executives those things that will create better alignment throughout the organization, as well as things that executives may not want to hear.

4. Managers and employees who don't align with the company's vision, values, and goals should be encouraged to adapt or leave the company. It is to their benefit to work within a culture for which they are better suited.

5. After undergoing extensive interviews, independent assessments, and reference checking, prospective candidates should be hired only if their personal dreams, purpose, values, and goals are aligned with the company's vision, mission, values and goals.

When done well, this five-step process guarantees that the team is aligned, committed, and working in the same direction. This is a true combination for success. Put it in your playbook.

CASE STUDY

A printing and graphic design firm had 20 employees, 3 departmental managers, and 2 executives (the CEO/owner and the COO). This business was hit hard by the recession in 2008-2009. Sales were declining as the industry became more digital. Morale was low. The CEO/owner had a sales background so it was hard for him to think about business strategy and the culture of his company—his focus was strictly on numbers and sales volume. Luckily, the COO had more leadership training and a background in organizational development.

The two executives needed to address their roles as the organization's leadership. It was especially difficult for the CEO, but eventually he learned how to more effectively delegate and feel less overwhelmed. Together, they defined a new vision for the company through their own ideas and client feedback.

They then created a set of values based on what they observed being practiced by employees within the company. They noted what behaviors demonstrated those values, what behaviors violated those values, and what actions they would take in response to those violations. This exercise allowed them to lead with one voice.

Lastly, they created a plan that encompassed four strategic initiatives in these areas: 1) sales and marketing; 2) innovation; 3) customer appreciation; and 4) employees and culture. Quarterly goals were set for each area.

The new plan was rolled out to employees during a company-sponsored event in which "summertime at the beach"-themed activities were mixed with serious conversations. There were games and prizes interspersed with small group feedback sessions and suggestion cards.

Many good ideas came out of the event and people were encouraged to take ownership of them. The CEO and COO were surprised and excited by the favorable response and level of engagement the employees exhibited after a long period of declining morale.

After the event, an online assessment was conducted to gauge employee attitudes in seven areas: planning, communication, customer support, benefits, leadership, measurement, and processes. The assessment revealed that while there were some areas of discontent, there were other areas in which the staff thought the company was doing a good job.

This assessment was followed by an 8-week development process for the three department managers. This addressed communication to those above and below them in the organization's hierarchy, micromanagement and delegation, making decisions, dealing with problem employees, how to coach to bring out the best in people, teamwork, motivation and developing leaders on their teams.

Weekly individual coaching helped each manager put these concepts to work on a daily basis. More delegation and teamwork ensued. More knowledge was shared as more cross training happened. Load balancing occurred giving people greater work/life balance. Morale improved as the managers got better at coaching.

Next, they ran another 8-week developmental process for the other employees, which focused on customer loyalty. During this time, each person developed his own personal dreams, purpose, values, and goals. Most became more intentional about how they were going after things they wanted in their lives and how their work dovetailed with that. In fact, as a result of this soul searching, one employee realized his desire to start his own business. He left the company to pursue his own dream, which opened up a spot for a new hire whose goals were more aligned with the company's goals.

As these developmental processes continued, employees began creating new ideas and working together on a self-initiating basis to improve workflow, increase productivity, enhance customer service, meet deadlines, and provide support to fellow co-workers. These acts of cooperation with and contribution to the team really made a difference. Even clients noted the change as the products delivered were more error free, completed on schedule, and handled by a happier customer service rep.

The company then integrated newer technologies for direct mail and digital processes that expanded the types of work they could produce for their clients. As employees saw how these changes were in line with their personal goals, they actively joined in the training process reducing the learning curve for the whole company. In turn, revenues increased without having to add another sales person.

The employees fully experienced how their dreams, purpose, values, and goals aligned with that of management, resulting in increased sales revenues, profitability, and a more fun and engaging work environment.

In fact, when the CEO and COO ran the same culture assessment the following year, satisfaction in all areas had drastically increased.

PLAYBOOK IDEAS: HOW CAN YOU APPLY THIS TO YOUR ORGANIZATION?

1. Many employers say that their people are their greatest asset, but then never invest in developing that asset to perform at the highest level. Business owners invest in many things—machinery service contracts, mailing lists, research and development—always trying to pinpoint the return on the investment. What return on investment could you expect by investing in developmental processes for your employees?

2. How can you make your managers aware of the importance of their sandwich roles as alignment translators and communicators?

3. Ask the following questions of each employee: Do you feel that your manager is a good coach? Does he have your best interest in mind? Does he set you up for discovery, learning, success, and growth? Can you go to him when you need support?

4. Ask your employees individually or in a group: What are the company's vision and mission?

5. Ask your employees individually or in a group: What are the company's values? If they can name them without reading from a list, ask them to share company stories that show a value in action.

6. Ask all your managers what they perceive to be the company's strategic initiatives. How many different answers do you get?

7. How can your executive team better communicate the company's vision, mission, values, and short and long-term goals so that others in the company receive and understand this information? It's more than just putting it out there—it must be heard and become actionable.

8. Do those who recruit and hire your employees (in-house or outsourced) investigate whether the candidate's dreams, purpose, values, and goals are aligned with your company's vision, mission, values, and goals? How can you take measures to ensure that this exploration becomes part of the hiring process?

Additional supportive material and opportunities for growth can be found at www.customerloyaltyplaybook.com

CHAPTER 5
THE COMPETENCY/
PREFERENCE MATRIX

preferences

	Activities I Love	Activities I Don't Mind Doing	Activities I Dislike
Activities I'm Really Good At	1	3	6
Activities I'm OK At	2	4	8
Activities That I'm Poor At	5	7	9

(left axis label: competencies)

Customer loyalty is earned by having everyone in the company fully engaged in their roles and fully invested in delighting the customer. Employee engagement is a big problem throughout the country and the world. Studies say that approximately two-thirds of employees are not engaged. How can you avoid that happening in your company?

The Competency/Preference Matrix is a tool that can be used in your Playbook to map out a game strategy for hiring the right people in positions that leverage their passions, strengths, and talents. In so doing, the employees will bring their best to a job they enjoy, the business owner can maximize her investment in the salary being paid, and the customers can deal with someone who truly loves what he is doing. It's a win-win-win for everybody.

Everyone has tasks that are easy for them, tasks that they are just okay at, and tasks that they do not do well. These are on the vertical axis of this matrix. Across the horizontal axis are preferences: activities that they love, don't mind doing, or dislike altogether.

The things that I love and am also good at are my special talents. These are things that put me in a state of flow. I do them effortlessly and don't even notice that time is passing. I feel fulfilled, enthusiastic, and full of energy. I look forward to getting up in the morning just so that I can engage in these activities. These are the activities that I can put in box #1 in the matrix. They are my unique abilities. In a perfect world, you and all of your employees would only do tasks that fell into box #1 for each of you.

Let's consider box #9. These are tasks that you hate and at which you feel incompetent. Performing these tasks is like pulling teeth. They take twice as long to complete because you don't like doing them, you don't do them well, and they don't come easily. So you spend two hours doing a job that someone else could do in half the time, with greater precision or know-how, and achieve a better result. Because you hate doing them, they drain your energy and leave you less able to do other things you need to do. The results you are generating are probably those of a novice rather than an expert who can approach the task with ease.

In the matrix, activities that fall into boxes 2, 3 and 4 are those with which you are familiar and can do fairly well. But they don't draw out your passion or capitalize on your unique abilities. You are mediocre at these activities. If I'm a business owner and my people are all functioning in boxes 2, 3, and 4, I may be running a pretty mediocre business.

Tasks that fall into boxes 5, 6, 7, and 8 are almost as bad as the #9 tasks. They are not being done well and most likely need to be reworked. Over time they create resentment and discontent in the people being asked to perform against their natural abilities and preferences.

THE SMALL BUSINESS OWNER AND DELEGATION

The typical entrepreneur starts a business and does everything himself because he lacks the resources to hire anybody. As his business grows, he may be reluctant to give up control for fear that no one else can handle the tasks better than he can. In truth, by attempting to do everything himself, he will probably become the worst boss he ever had.

Here's a scenario I've seen often. How many small business owners really know bookkeeping? Sure, they can get to know the basics if they take a course on QuickBooks, follow a manual, or get help from a friend. But they would really benefit from using a person who specializes in bookkeeping, who knows QuickBooks inside out, and uses it every day, to say nothing about the accounting knowledge that helps them organize the right financial data more accurately to get management reports that really contribute to business growth. If this function were delegated to someone for whom bookkeeping were a #1 task instead of a #9 task, it would be done in half the time and with fewer errors. There would be better management reports yielding better decision-making.

Another example is website creation. Many small business owners try to be their own webmasters or give the job to someone in their company who knows a little about it. The popular thinking is that if they learn the intricacies of WordPress or HTML, they will save money or maintain control. This is an illusion. It costs more money because of the time taken away from revenue generating activities. It also robs the small business of the professionalism in design and programming that an experienced web designer or programmer can provide. Again the small business owner is not only wasting his manpower and financial resources, but also creating an inferior product.

If the small business owner were to delegate either of these functions to someone who did them as a #1 talent and passion, there would be more fulfillment, less time wasted, and a better outcome.

USING THE MATRIX WITH EMPLOYEES

The best use of the matrix is to help your employees identify their ideal current and future positions within your firm. When your employees are working in their #1 box, they are happy and super-productive. They are using their unique abilities to effortlessly create success after success. Your culture will improve and morale will be high. The resulting happiness and fulfillment will contribute to an improved customer experience and increase both staff and client loyalty.

The Competency/Preference Matrix is a way of honing in on all the things you or your employees do and categorizing them so that you can delegate the work more effectively and efficiently. Putting people in positions that draw on their natural talents and passions multiplies your business and turns your team into A-players, exactly what you need for a winning game plan.

In putting the matrix to work with your employees, start with these four steps:

1. The best way to get started with this matrix is to have each person list all the things he does each day, week, and month. Have your employees list their daily tasks from email and phone calls to meetings and managing others. It should cover every task that gets done. Make each one a specific action item and make it start with a verb. List weekly and monthly activities as well.
2. Put the list of activities into a two-column spreadsheet. In the second column of the spreadsheet label each task with the number of the square of the Competency/Preference Matrix that that task represents for the doer, numbers 1 through 9.
3. Then he can use the spreadsheet's "sort" function to order the tasks by the number column. All the #1's will be grouped together as well as all the # 9's.

4. Decision making time. Does the person have a preponderance of #1 tasks? If so, he is in a great position for being on top of his game. Or are the majority of tasks rated higher than 4? This means he isn't right for the position he is in and you, as the business owner or HR professional, need to find him a different role that matches his strengths and passions. If you do not have that type of position available, you can help him find employment where he will use his passions and strengths. In the end, he will be happier and you will be able to hire someone who has preferences and competencies that match the available job more successfully.

You can use this matrix to guide career paths and give promotions to people in your organization. As people evaluate their options for promotion and future career planning, competencies can be developed and preferences tested using the matrix as a structure for planning and evaluation. Many companies give bigger "stretch" projects to people coming up through the ranks so that these individuals can try what they like, show off their strengths, and develop skills to position themselves for the future.

USING THIS MATRIX IN A JOB INTERVIEW

The list of tasks can also be used to create a job description from which you can recruit the right employee. The best candidate to hire is the one whose #1 tasks (most loved and most competent at) are the ones needed by the company for this role based on the job description. Many entrepreneurs automatically want to hire someone just like himself or herself. But this is not what is needed. The person that should be hired needs to like what he does *and* have the right mix of skills so that tasks will be accomplished with speed and ease.

You can also provide this matrix to prospective candidates during a job interview. Share it with the candidate and then ask: "Using this matrix, what are some activities that fall into square #1 for you?" or "In your last job, what squares did your responsibilities fall into?" If the #1's that he describes is similar to the tasks you need done, that's an indication that he may be a good candidate.

CASE STUDY

Jack has a technology firm that creates software solutions and mobile apps. He loves to immerse himself into the development of new industry-leading products. His company has been growing rapidly and he keeps adding people to handle the load. With 40 people on staff, it is becoming a challenge to manage them all. There is so much going on, so many new and existing clients to manage, and so many products being developed, that it is difficult to keep it all straight. Not everyone is effective in their roles since they keep getting switched around. Some people are getting tired of being moved to new projects just as they are feeling competent with the one they are currently working on. Things are starting to fall through the cracks. Furthermore, Jack loves to hire people like himself who are great technologists. He enjoys talking with them over coffee about the intricacies of certain kinds of coding and, before you know it, they are on the team contributing to the R&D. To complicate matters, parts of the company are not informed about what the *other* parts are doing. There is duplication of effort, lack of communication, unnecessary competition, lack of administrative support to track versioning and protect intellectual property, and often insufficient communication with the customer who actually commissioned the product creation.

I suggested that Jack have his employees list all their duties on individual spreadsheets over a one-week time period. They assigned numbers from the Competency/Preference Matrix to each task they performed. We also conducted assessments that pinpointed each person's strengths. Jack and several of his most trusted managers looked over the spreadsheets and assessment reports of the employees. We started mapping people into the roles for which they were best suited. We then interviewed each employee, showing them the results of the assessment and how it matched up to the competencies and preferences they had identified. We created a position for each one (some similar and some different than the position currently held) with a career development path.

Jack and his team got the buy-in from each employee and reduced costly turnover. Sometimes compromises were made. But overall, out of the chaos, came a structure of service, support, R&D, client relations, and people in the right roles to suit their preferences and competencies. Each person now had a clear career development path, which resulted in more stability for the company and a more stable workforce. It also provided a structure for future hires. Not only did the company retain its employees in a very competitive market, but it also received a lucrative acquisition offer the following year, which made Jack very happy.

PLAYBOOK IDEAS: HOW CAN YOU APPLY THIS TO YOUR ORGANIZATION?

1. Have each person in your company list his daily activities over the course of a week. Include phone calls, meetings, reports, and everything else accomplished during that period. Add to the list activities done on a weekly or monthly basis. Apply the Competency/Preference Matrix numbering system to each of the tasks.

2. Compute the average number for each employee. Is it closer to a 1 or a 9? If it's 4, 5, 6, 7, 8 or 9, that person is probably in the wrong role and you are wasting the money invested in his employment. Can you switch that person to a different role where the activities are 1, 2, or 3 for him?

3. Sometimes people have a high preference but low competency (#5) for a particular role. That's an invitation to provide them with additional training so they show an even better ROI for the money you've already invested in them. Who do you have working for you who is in this position?

4. Sometimes people have a high competency in an area but a low preference (#6). Is the work too easy? Do they need a challenge? Are they burned out? Dig deeper to find the true cause and renew their passion. Maybe you'll find a superstar.

5. After making certain that your employees are using their unique abilities in a mutually beneficial way, how can you provide them with a career path that will keep them employed over time and maximize your investment in them?

6. What if you discover that someone you like really isn't in the right role for his competencies and preferences? What if you don't currently have another position for that person? Will you create something new or allow them to create their own role? Or will you graciously help them find a position elsewhere where their unique talents can be fully developed?

7. Keep your awareness of the human side. Each employee is not only an investment, but is also someone who is unique and special. How can you create balance between your personal emotional connections as well as the financial investment in each employee?

Additional supportive material and opportunities for growth can be found at www.customerloyaltyplaybook.com

the Skills Curve

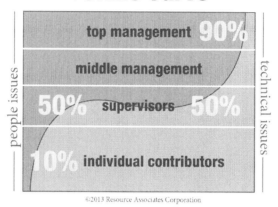

©2013 Resource Associates Corporation

Inserted with permission
Copyrighted by Resource Associates Corporation

Your employees, depending on their positions, have both people skills and technical skills. What do I mean by technical skills? I'm referring to the work of the company—accounting if it's an accounting firm, doing the actual auto repair in a car repair shop, or creating engineering drawings in an engineering company. What are the people skills? Connecting empathetically with customers, working collaboratively with colleagues, staying calm when tempers are flaring, being able to take direction without getting defensive, giving instructions clearly, communicating so that the other person buys into what you're saying, providing inspiration and motivation to others, and being fair and caring.

The Skills Curve graphic above shows that as a group, *individual contributors* (noted at the bottom of the chart) rely heavily on technical skills to do their jobs. Their people skills are used only 10% of the time and mostly to interact with their colleagues. If they work in a service-based company, they may also interact with customers. However, their jobs are primarily focused on doing the actual work of the company in providing a product or service.

When an individual contributor is promoted to supervisor, his skill shift is significant. The new role now demands at least 50% people skills and 50% technical skills. As supervisor, he will have to give instructions clearly, oversee a staff (comprised of former peers), be able to motivate and inspire them to be productive, and handle whatever personal or emotional issues arise for his subordinates in the work environment. He will also have to handle conflict between employees or emotions around the company's management.

Supervisors take direction from their managers and communicate these directions to their teams. They are now in the sandwich position of having to align the vision, values, and goals of the company with those of the people they supervise.

They also communicate employee feedback and input to the upper layers of management. They advocate for their staff to ensure that each person gets a fair deal. They make more decisions with higher impact. They have a higher level of responsibility and are accountable for results from others.

Without proper training and development, many newly promoted supervisors fail to make the transition. Why? First of all, the best technician may not be the best person to promote, as he may not have the requisite people skills, nor be willing to learn them. Secondly, the company could really lose out if this person fails. Not only does it lose a star technician, it loses a supervisor, too.

It is wiser to develop and train a few top contenders at the individual contributor level and see who excels at people skills and leadership, and then promote that candidate into the supervisor position based on skills needed for the new role. Additional training, development, and coaching should be given to the new supervisor to make her even more effective as she comes up against everyday challenges. This provides a greater guarantee of success for the new supervisor and for the whole team.

Moving up through the chart, we come to the *middle* and *top management* levels. These leaders handle even more people-related issues. They motivate, communicate, make decisions, pull together teams, coach, and collaborate. They interact with clients and industry partners. They make policy decisions affecting many people. The choices they make determine who the ideal clients are, how the work gets done (and by whom), what benefits are provided to employees, how the company's culture will evolve, and how to identify and create advantageous alliances. They determine the company's vision, values, and goals, and then communicate them to the rest of the company. These are larger-scale issues that have little in common with the technical work done by the individual contributors.

Middle and top management positions also require greater emotional intelligence and sensitivity to people issues. They need strategic thinking, a risk-taking entrepreneurial spirit, and a vision of what success could be like. The important decisions made by these managers set precedents that can underlie monumental shifts in other people's lives and families. Leaders at the top of organizations are not as swayed by day-to-day concerns; they are focused on a bigger picture and strategies for achieving long-term goals.

When being promoted from supervisor to middle management and then to top management, a change in mindset is required. The higher the position in the organization, the more responsibility. "The buck stops here" mentality characterizes top management. They also become leaders outside their companies, getting recognition from their industries or communities. They network extensively to create alliances with strategic partners and customers.

Without appropriate training and development, many of these leaders will fail to progress. The "Peter Principal" of rising to one's level of incompetence often comes into play.

Enhancing relationship skills is crucial and productive. The most successful leaders attend training programs, mastermind mentoring groups, improvisational theater or storytelling workshops, emotional intelligence presentations, and other development programs to enhance their leadership potential.

One of the biggest deterrents to company growth is the inability of its CEO to grow and engage in big picture thinking. A company owner who doesn't plan or expand the culture of his company, who doesn't hold his managers accountable for their actions, and who doesn't take the customer experience seriously holds his company back.

Successful company owners are aware of these stumbling blocks to success and constantly seek self-improvement. They continue their education through academic as well as entrepreneur programs. They understand that the time and money invested in self-development pays big dividends in the long run. By developing themselves they are upgrading the engine that propels the company forward. Leadership growth is a game strategy with guaranteed value.

CASE STUDY

John, a building contractor, worked for the city of New York after Hurricane Sandy swept through. John had about 25 workers out in the field and about 5 workers in the office. He put in about 80 hours a week.

The city required lots of paperwork in order to be eligible to bid for jobs and even more paperwork when given a contract. There were many rules and regulations governing the use of subcontractors, job safety, handling materials, and getting proper approvals from all the parties involved. John was personally handling all the compliances and paperwork, but he soon fell behind on this responsibility. This failure to meet paperwork deadlines created a big problem for the company and John became the bottleneck.

Fortunately, the city ran programs and classes on how to get these jobs and how to complete the paperwork necessary. John attended these classes and, upon completion, enrolled in another course to learn about marketing, management, systems, finances, leadership, and strategic planning. He then invested in a one-on-one coaching and consulting to apply this knowledge to his team and to create a long-term business plan for his company beyond his current jobs. He knew that while there was plenty of work, he should take advantage of every opportunity to grow his business and get a head start for a sustainable future.

Our work together helped John build infrastructure, hire the right people, and develop his company's vision, values, and strategic initiatives. He came to understand that he could delegate tasks and didn't have to be the bottleneck. His hunger for knowledge and a desire to learn took him to the next level in business leadership. He landed more contracts and made more money on each one increasing his revenues 50%. This also allowed him to spend more quality time with his family and to kick back and relax.

PLAYBOOK IDEAS: HOW CAN YOU APPLY THIS TO YOUR ORGANIZATION?

1. Are you the bottleneck in your company? Do tasks get held up waiting for you to get to them all?

2. How can you do more working *on* your business instead of *in* your business? In other words, how can you spend more time focusing on the business's strategies and growth, instead of the work of the business? Can you delegate to someone else? You'll be really stuck until you do.

3. What would be the impact if your company provided training and development for employees at every level?

4. When promoting an employee, do you mostly consider whether their skills are best suited for the new position . . . or, rather, how well they performed in the job they are leaving? How would you know what their future performance might be?

5. How could behavioral and competency assessments be helpful when making decisions about promotions? How could "stretch" projects be helpful to you in pinpointing people ready for promotion? (A "stretch" project is a short-term project outside a person's job description, to acquire and showcase new skills.)

6. The chart above shows a shift from technical capabilities to people capabilities between the individual contributor and supervisor levels. In your organization, is there a point where the need for people skills surpasses the need for technical skills? If you're promoting from within, how does your company help people make that shift?

7. Are you a manager looking to get a promotion? If so, are you willing to take responsibility for developing into a major player? What leadership training and development opportunities could you be utilizing (even on a self-pay basis) to become the person you need to be to earn that promotion?

Additional supportive material and opportunities for growth can be found at www.customerloyaltyplaybook.com

CHAPTER 7
COMFORT ZONE BUBBLE

A comfort zone is like a bubble. It is a mindset around and about yourself that defines what's comfortable and convenient for you to do. It is the behavioral equivalent of your identity. Business owners often get used to seeing and doing things in a certain way. They develop habits and these habits can become limiting. For example, when it comes to customer service, many business owners are willing to maintain the status quo based on previous experience. It is then difficult to come up with new ideas that are outside the comfort zone of their own private bubble.

Stretching to do the unfamiliar, trying out something new, or adopting a new model is not the default for our brains. Our brains have created neural pathways reinforced by repeated usage. To think or behave a different way requires neuroplasticity. New neural pathways need to be created that abandon old habits and start reinforcing new ones. This results in a shift in comfort zone or personal bubble.

To fully understand this concept, try this exercise. Cross your arms in front of your stomach. Which arm is on top? Now try this position with the other arm on top. Does it feel foreign and uncomfortable? That's because your brain is wired to have neural pathways that feel comfortable in the first pattern and uncomfortable in the second pattern.

How do we develop these patterns in the first place? We adopt behaviors early in life by modeling them after our parents. Life circumstances reinforce our patterns. Our strongest learned pattern is the one that forms our initial reaction to any situation. There are many ways to react to any event. Because of our upbringing, we react in a particular way. For instance, some people react to rudeness by getting equally as rude.

How does this apply to how we handle our clients? Some of our customers will be rude or mean and for a variety of reasons. If we react out of defensive behavior patterns, we will make things worse, not better. We can react, instead, by wondering what made that person act rudely. Is he having a bad day? Did something happen to that person that requires our empathy?

Consider this story. A man is on a train accompanied by several children and an older man who appears to be the grandfather. The children are acting out, being loud and obnoxious, and disrupting the other passengers. The father is oblivious to all the commotion. He just sits and stares. The passengers wonder: *Why doesn't the father do something? Why doesn't he control his kids?* They are annoyed and bothered. The train soon arrives at a stop and the family gets up to leave. As they are leaving, the grandfather turns to the passengers and says, "Please forgive my family. My son buried his wife today and the children's lives have been turned upside down without their mother." This evokes an immediate change in the other passengers. Their thoughts of annoyance turn to sympathy. Their internal state changes from irritation to compassion. This change of state can happen in an instant.

Being able to consider the state of mind of a customer and then alter your mental state accordingly is a skill that anyone handling customers needs to have. You may be dealing with someone who is difficult, so being empathetic and in control will help the situation and prepare you for the next customer encounter.

We are human and the patterns we develop throughout our lives play out in the way we treat customers. How could your own mood or attitude affect the customer experience? Perhaps things didn't go well this morning. Your kids missed the bus or you had an argument with your spouse. You're now late to work and you have to park further away. You come into the office in a state of agitation, stress, and negativity, wondering: *What else is going to go wrong today?* This is not the state of mind that is conducive to handling customer requests or dealing with the various moods customers will bring to today's interactions. The same goes for your co-workers.

You are, however, fully capable of changing your mental state. You can shift to a state of calm positivity by breathing deeply and regularly. Other exercises include meditating, remembering funny things, playing music you like, and thinking about someone who really cares about you. You can change your negative context to an empowering one. This capacity to change grows with practice like a muscle grows through exercise. It expands your comfort zone.

STIMULUS → THOUGHT → RESPONSE

Airline flight attendants have customer-centric jobs in a potentially stressful environment, so they are properly trained to handle emergencies. If a flight attendant is on a plane that is in trouble, she is naturally fearful for her own life. This can put her in panic mode and unable to handle the emotional needs of the passengers.

To keep her priorities in focus, she is trained to grab a pillow to help suspend her own fear and put her back into rational thinking so she can stay calm for the other passengers.

If she just reacts, the stimulus (fear of plane going down) produces a response (panic and fear). Stimulus → Response. However, if she grabs a pillow to interrupt her immediate reaction, the impact of the stimulus weakens, allowing a rational thought (my job is to be helpful) to replace it, which results in a different response (I will take care of my passengers). Stimulus → Thought → Response.

In dealing with customers, clients, and fellow employees, we all have emotions that get triggered and buttons that get pushed. We also have bad days in which we have to deal with negative situations more often than we would prefer. To remain cool and unflustered, to handle it all with diplomacy, to be empathetic, and to create positive solutions no matter how high the emotions are flying, if you remember *Stimulus → Thought → Response*, you can create an empowering context that achieves results.

In essence this is a game plan that empowers all your other game plans. For an athlete it's to remain cool under pressure and to not let his emotions disrupt the play. It's the same in your business. You can have lots of plans and strategies. They are going to be accomplished by people. If people's uncontrolled emotional responses get in the way, the plans may be sabotaged.

HANDLING COMPLAINTS: LISTEN, THANK, APOLOGIZE, TAKE ACTION

How about an empowering context around a complaint? When you get a complaint, it's a gift. Unlike most customers, the complainer has taken the time to tell you about something that isn't right. It's a chance to fix the problem that you wouldn't have had if he had never contacted you. This customer cares. Respond by using this four-step process:

1. *Listen* to him completely. He will be easier to deal with if he feels you *hear* his problem and he's gotten to vent his emotions. Plus, you'll learn something valuable.
2. *Thank* him for bringing the problem to your attention. He just increased your income and helped you do a better job.
3. *Apologize.* He has been inconvenienced by the faulty product/service and now by having to contact you.
4. *Take action.* Make the situation right. Customer loyalty gets deepened when customers feel taken care of when things go wrong. It creates "how they fixed it" stories that promote positive word-of-mouth.

Your comfort zone bubble expands when it contains more solutions and options for problem solving. It includes handling emotional issues around people who have problems that seem insurmountable. It includes conscious listening, compassion, and apologizing. It becomes all about the customer and not about the mood of the person serving the client.

Expanding the comfort zone bubble is a necessary skill at every level in a company. A manager expands her comfort zone by adjusting to a new view of the organization. The staff that handle clients expands their comfort zones by learning to shift their mental states. They can also use Stimulus → Thought → Response instead of just reacting. When employees see a complaint as a gift, they can create higher levels of customer loyalty.

CASE STUDY

Dan owns a 50-person technology company that installs and maintains computer and phone networks for small and midsize businesses. He started the company on his own as a technician and has gradually added employees over the last five years. In the early days he thought of himself as a solo entrepreneur with a few helpers. He was encouraged to hire people smarter than himself, but he was very resistant to that idea. After all, how could he supervise them well if they were more tech savvy than he was? He was comfortable in his tech zone bubble while occasionally dabbling in the role of business owner when necessary.

One day, Dan landed a big contract. There was no way he could handle the new project with only a few techs in training. He had to hire some big guns or else the contract wouldn't be managed well. He started interviewing and the process was uncomfortable. It was hard asking questions of those who had been in the industry longer, handled bigger networks, or had more experience with routers and servers that he had ever had. Eventually, when Dan realized that this was *his* business and he had to run it like a businessperson, not like a tech, the process became easier. He had to greatly expand his comfort zone to feel more at ease in this new role of business owner.

During one particular interview with a potential candidate who had vast experience and excellent credentials, Dan began to feel humbled, disempowered, and somewhat defensive over this candidate's capabilities and the awards he had won. At one point in the interview, the candidate asked Dan how it felt to be a business owner, handling customers and their payments, and dealing with risk and the unpredictability of work, especially when the economy wasn't doing well. Something shifted in Dan at that moment. He was doing well and managing his cash, growing his business, and creating jobs in his community. He realized the candidate, who he greatly respected, had no desire to be an entrepreneur. The candidate's comfort zone did not include risk whereas that was easy for Dan. Dan's confidence increased with this new awareness. His comfort zone as an entrepreneur increased. This revelation freed him to make empowering decisions about organizing workflow and attracting more clients and highly skilled staff.

PLAYBOOK IDEAS: HOW CAN YOU APPLY THIS TO YOUR ORGANIZATION?

1. Describe some situations (work or home) where a comfort zone bubble is apparent and where people don't do what's outside their comfort zones.
2. How has your comfort zone limited you? How do you react when someone challenges you to do or be something outside your comfort zone bubble?
3. What methods do you and your employees use to master personal emotions and change from a bad mood to a good mood in just a moment or two? When is this helpful?
4. Can you recall when you changed your state from a negative to an empowering one? What did you do or think about that made a difference?
5. In which situations have you been unable to change your mental state?
6. Are there particular customers or customer situations that you and your staff find challenging? How can you expand your comfort zones to find better solutions—ones that would make the customer feel better as well as solve the problem?
7. Role-play handling a complaint. Practice the *Listen, Thank, Apologize, Take Action* scenario so that it is ingrained in your employees' minds. It's easy to get defensive or try to look good, but that's exactly the wrong way to get results.

Additional supportive material and opportunities for growth can be found at www.customerloyaltyplaybook.com

CUSTOMER EXPERIENCE

CHAPTER 8
CUSTOMERS ON YOUR VACATIONS

When we go on vacation, we go with family or friends that we know we'll enjoy. Of course, there are exceptions. We may not like certain family members or the friend of a friend that happens to come along, too. But, by and large, we're planning an enjoyable experience with people close to us with whom we have bonds, derive meaningful conversations, and have had pleasant past experiences. Each friend or family member has his or her own personality, quirks, strengths, weaknesses, interests, style, etc., and each person elicits from us a different kind of empathy. Even if we don't recognize it in the moment, it's important to point out what we see and relate to each other in a special and unique way.

Research conducted by Gallop polls and McKinsey studies shows that clients don't remain loyal to your business just because you provide them with reasonable or even great transactional customer service. That's just the minimum. Customers keep coming back and become your raving fans because you also have developed personal relationships with them that reflect trust, communication, and an empathetic connection. Together, you're creating a shared experience that you can bond over—just like a journey together or a pleasant vacation. You often find commonalities with each customer that reinforces how unique you are—not just as a talking business-head at the other end of the phone, but also as a real person with families, pets, cares, likes, and dislikes of your own. This is communicated by the warm tone of your voice, the eye contact (if you're face-to-face), the way you ask questions and listen for an answer, your ability to laugh and be playful, and how you show you care.

Wouldn't it be great if while we're talking with a client, they have the delightful experience that they are "on vacation" with us? If you want your client to feel that way, view him as a person that could potentially go on vacation with you. (If that's too difficult, view the person as someone who goes on vacation with his own family.)

Let's look at aspects of the vacation experience and see how it can be applied to the relationships we have with clients.

THE SENSORY EXPERIENCE

One of my favorite places to go on vacation with my family is the shore. We enjoy going to the beach together, feeling the warmth of the sun and the coolness of the water. We go to our favorite ice cream parlor where the servers sing and dance and the ice cream is rich and creamy. We hit a bar or two and listen to music. We play pinochle and tease each other about how we're playing. We cook meals together and enjoy the sunsets on the deck.

Did you notice the sensory experiences detailed in this description? There was the sand, the sun, and the water (feeling); ice cream (tasting); music and pinochle chit-chat (hearing); playing cards and the sunset (seeing); and cooking meals together (smelling). The way our brains have evolved, when we experience something through our senses and the sensory experience is associated with positive emotions, we remember it a long time. We may not recall the actual details of these interactions, but we do remember the sensory experiences and how positive the person or event associated with the sensory memory, made us feel.

How can we create sensory experiences during a customer's buying experience? Most retail stores know how to do this well. Some play music in the background; others use aromatherapy through scented candles or potpourri. Bookstores offer snacks and comforting drinks. Many stores arrange their inventory in colorful, well-designed displays that catch your eye or use soothing lighting. Some businesses provide food or wine tastings. Restaurants pump pleasant food aromas into the air outside the restaurant.

Companies also use sensory experiences to create the "vacation experience" with their employees. In many ways, employees are a company's internal customers. As such, they are offered free lunches or invited to annual picnics and holiday parties so that both employees and management can bond while enjoying casual time together. This encourages employee retention.

In your situation, how can you incorporate a sensory component that will enhance the client relationship? No matter how professional you think you need to be, remember, we're all human and respond to our senses unconsciously.

REPEATABLE TRADITION

Every time my family returns to our usual shore location, we reinforce our past experience of enjoying it together. It becomes something we share over and over and it strengthens the bonds we have with each other. Going to the ice cream parlor, for instance, generates conversations of "remember when we were here last year," who sang what song, what we ate, how hard we laughed, who was with us, and what has changed. We now have this year's memory layered on last year's memory and all the layers of years before that. The bonds grow stronger with every layer.

How can we incorporate layered and positive emotional traditions in our clients' experiences? We can recall memories of things we talk about each time we come in contact. Companies that have CRM (customer relationship management) software can record notes about conversations, client preferences, birthdays, etc. Remembering that Pat likes to talk about her cat and bringing it up the next time you get her on the phone reinforces the pleasurable first conversation. Taking a client to a sporting event, an art opening, or a nonprofit fundraiser creates shared experiences. When repeated, these experiences become a tradition with multi-layered bonding.

THE INCLUSION FACTOR

When new friends come along on our family's vacations, they get swept up in the camaraderie. We share our memories with our friends and wind up explaining what originally happened. This generates various versions of the same story, a lot of discussion, and a retelling of the traditions, which increases our bonds. The new person becomes part of the fun and part of our network. As she contributes to the present experience, she also becomes a new component in the evolving tradition. This is part of the vacation experience--the group coalescing and magnifying the experience of those who are present even if they don't yet share all the traditions.

People are social animals and have a deep emotional need to belong. They want to feel included and valued by the group. Being able to contribute and getting recognized for that contribution is an active form of building social bonds. When companies run charity

CHAPTER 8 CUSTOMERS ON YOUR VACATIONS

walks or community service days and ask their customers, employees, and vendors to get involved, they are building community, belonging, and inclusion. These bonds create commitment and loyalty much in the same way as going on vacation together.

Another example of building inclusion in our clients' experiences is to have a client appreciation event where your clients can bring guests. The clients will talk to each other and reinforce their experiences with your firm. The prospects will get caught up in the momentum and enthusiasm and actively look at becoming your client as well.

If your business targets a specific industry and then becomes a sponsor of an industry event, the guests are most likely existing clients and some prospects. If your existing clients recount stories of the traditions they've shared with you and your company, the prospects become engaged and interested. This will enhance their experience at the event and possibly inspire them to develop their own positive and repeatable traditions with your firm.

Sports organizations have game plans. They build relatedness with their fans through giveaways of items that you can touch, feel or taste. They build traditions with music, slogans season tickets. They build a connection to star players through autographs, pictures and PR. They make the fans feel they belong through special events, contests and clothing. You can look at their strategies and see what you might adapt for your game strategy.

CASE STUDY

A company that develops and sells training curriculum and tools to consultants understands the concept of shared experiences. They have clients with whom they interact regularly on a multi-sensory level. They hold conferences that include food, music, laughter, and fun. Games are played and there are cook-offs to see who prepares the best chili or chocolate chip cookies. Participants attend wearing sports team clothing to create bonds and camaraderie. Everyone listens to and shares ideas and clients are given mementos to remind them of speeches delivered.

Because these conferences occur regularly, repeatable, layered traditions are established. People joke about an older consultant's non-use of technology or the way a very vocal but knowledgeable participant always has something to add. There is a late night bar that has been affectionately dubbed the "Knowledge Center" because of the informal sharing that happens over drinks.

When someone new attends one of the conferences, she gets caught up in the nostalgia of the repeatable traditions. Stories get related and sometimes embellished. This new person, Jane, gets brought into the culture. Her perceptions and expectations are partially shaped by the group consensus. Her participation becomes part of the repeated traditions of the next meeting when those that are present say "Remember what Jane said when she was first here?"

PLAYBOOK IDEAS: HOW CAN YOU APPLY THIS TO YOUR ORGANIZATION?

Think about how you can make your clients' experiences more like a vacation with your family so they will want to come back again and again. Brainstorm with your team and come up with ideas for the following:

1. Look at the way you interact with your customers and clients. What sensory experiences can you add to your customer interactions so that their emotional experiences with you are more memorable in their core brain functions (even subliminally)?
2. What repeatable experiences can you create so that there are multiple layers of relatedness?

3. How can you use the inclusion factor to include new prospects in your existing clients' web of bonds and traditions to maximize the quality of relationships and the quantity of raving fans?

4. Have your employees list all their favorite things to do when they are on vacation—swimming, hiking, art shows, racing, watching a sunset, sightseeing, going out to dinner, etc. Are there multiple people with the same interests? Plan an event for clients that incorporates those activities. For instance, if hiking is popular, plan a bus trip to a national park with hiking trails and invite your clients and staff to participate. Or plan a virtual hiking event game that clients can play with you.

5. Can you create an event for your clients and have them bring along guests that can, in turn, become new prospects? Perhaps a "customer appreciation" event where non-client guests are encouraged to attend? This type of event will enable new contacts to get caught up in the testimonials and enthusiasm of your clients.

6. Can you create a community event or sponsor a charitable event and use it to build an active sense of belonging with your clients, employees, and vendors?

7. What can you make happen regularly and repeatedly to create a positive history with your clients?

Additional supportive material and opportunities for growth can be found at www.customerloyaltyplaybook.com

CHAPTER 9
POC CIRCLES

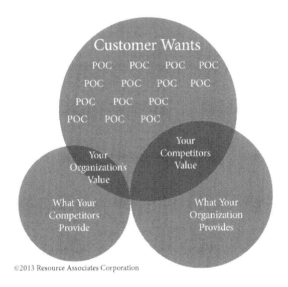

©2013 Resource Associates Corporation

Inserted with permission
Copyrighted by Resource Associates Corporation

In the last chapter we applied the elements of a vacation to enhance client experiences and connections. In this chapter we will continue exploring the depth of that connection, why people buy, and how we can define the experience more precisely.

What do your customers really want? Research done by Gallup, McKinsey, and Bain Consulting has shown that customers buy emotionally and then rationalize their purchases by logical thinking. Best-selling business author Simon Sinek says, "People don't buy *what* you do, they buy *why* you do it." That means the *why* behind your brand has more impact than the *what* (features and benefits) of the products you offer. People buy from the limbic parts of their brains where their emotions and decision-making are housed, not the neocortex part of their brains, which is the seat of rational and analytical thought. The neocortex, with its ability for language, comprehends features and benefits.

However, the limbic part of the brain, which has no capacity for language, drives behavior with gut feelings like trust, loyalty, fear, disappointment, joy, and inspiration. People buy because their gut "tells" them that they'll feel better having both the product and customer experience you offer. People want to feel loved, special, unique, deserving, and recognized. They want you to feel empathy for their situation. They want to know you are committed to their best interest and not to your own agenda. Each of these aspects of emotional connection is represented in the above graphic by a POC in the "Customer wants" circle. POC stands for *Point of Connection*.

Points of Connection provide much of the impetus for why people buy from your company, your sales force, and your customer service staff. Every time you, your team, or your brand interacts with a client, there's an opportunity to create greater emotional connection resulting in ever-increasing trust and loyalty. This is well recognized in the sales world. Salespeople understand that they need to build "know, like, and trust" with each prospect before any purchase will take place.

So what exactly is a POC? Points of connection are the customer touches made daily and in many ways: a phone call; an email; a face-to-face conversation; a letter; a marketing message; the moment a client enters your parking lot or your place of business; how customers interact with your product and packaging; your website's message/navigation/design; an article or blog post you've written; a presentation you made at a seminar or conference; word of mouth from friends and colleagues; the name on your truck; the candy left on a pillow at the hotel for your guests; and what is posted about you on Facebook, LinkedIn, Instagram, Pinterest or Yelp. Each of these interactions leads to positive or negative associations that build up like an emotional piggy bank inside the limbic parts of the brain. One coin in for a positive experience . . . often six coins out for something negative.

The more emotionally connecting experiences you create, the more coins you put in the piggy bank of customer loyalty. In other words, the more your circle of POCs overlaps with your prospect's circle of POCs, the more business they will do with you. Your competitors also overlap their POC circles with the prospect. To the extent that you can provide more and higher quality POCs than your competitor, you have an advantage.

What variables can improve a POC? As previously mentioned in Chapter 8, people receive data from the world through their five senses. We all know that a smile, eye contact, saying a client's name, and having a positive attitude can improve the quality of the interaction. But have you thought about these other POCs? How does the phone get answered? Is it a canned message or is it warm and alive, making the caller feel like it's the best thing that happened to her all day? Focusing on the customer as if she were the only person in the world makes her feel special. Every vocal or written interaction can communicate something unique about your relationship so that her limbic brain experiences, "I'm remembered. I matter. I have value. Someone thinks I'm special."

What about POCs that aren't written or vocal interactions? Many things will communicate your brand of caring and being there for the prospect. For example, how does your waiting room or entry area look? Is it clean, well designed, well lit, and welcoming? Is it easy getting into and out of the parking lot? Is there a pleasant smell in your store or office? Is the music calming, soothing, and inspiring? Many hotels now offer chocolate chip cookies or apples at the front desk. See how often you can enhance each POC through continuing to offer more stimulating sights, sounds, touch, smells, and tastes.

CONNECTING POCS TO LEADERSHIP AND EMPLOYEES

This is where many concepts in this book come together in the moment of truth—the customer interaction. In a customer-centric culture, leaders pay attention to the points of connection with both their customers and their employees. They hire only those people who have a focus on customer care. And they treat their employees with the same caring and respect that they expect their employees to exercise with their customers.

Strong leaders want employees that buy into the *why* of the company. They want employees that naturally align to the vision, values, and goals of the company. These leaders realize that their employees are the key to connecting with customers. As such, they develop their team members, deepen their awareness of how to connect, and expand their ability to connect. They push distributed leadership down into all the layers of the organization knowing that customers want hassle-free, immediate decisions. Every employee can be trained and empowered to make decisions that positively impact a customer's experience.

Leaders are aware that each employee wants the same love, caring, respect, attention, and feeling of being special and unique that every client wants. They connect with employees on this personal, approachable level just as they expect their employees to connect on a personal level with customers and prospects. They walk the talk and model the behavior.

These leaders value emotional intelligence. They work at deepening their own emotional intelligence, even if they came up through the ranks in an emotionally unintelligent organization. They continue their development by discovering blind spots, giving up past beliefs that no longer serve them, and working to become more emotionally aware. They know the ongoing success of their company depends on it.

This game strategy is all about caring. If you and your staff don't care and you're just going through the motions at each POC, every customer will see through it. Coaches' game strategies are to recruit athletes who care about thriving on a team, who care about and respect themselves, who have 'fire in the belly' to win, who care about the quality of the role model they portray. The caring gives a foundation to creating and implementing fan generating POCs.

CASE STUDY

Let's take the case of Zappos, an online shoe retailer. CEO Tony Hsieh, in his book *Delivering Happiness* says, "We're not a shoe company that happens to give great customer service; we're a service company that happens to sell shoes." He has also said in an *Inc.* magazine article, "We believe that forming personal, emotional connections with our customers is the best way to provide great service."

His company is famous for their superb customer service policies. For instance, they take hiring and training very seriously because they only want people on board who are dedicated to great customer service. Candidates go through a rigorous interview and assessment process and are selected according to very high standards. Then, they are put through a month of training. No matter what the position, all new hires must spend part of that training time waiting on customers via phone. About a week into the training, each trainee is offered $2,000 to leave the company. People that value their customer service role more highly than any monetary reward are the people Zappos wants in its organization. If they take the money, these candidates actually save the company many more thousands of dollars in wasted training and development.

Zappos is very aware of its Points of Connection with customers. They frequently upgrade the shipping to overnight delivery. They've been known to send flowers to customers, when circumstances warrant. There is no time limit on the length of phone calls with clients. Their employees comment online about their culture and their values. They show pictures of their highly decorated and customized workspaces. Employees are free to make decisions without having to get approval.

The following is a great example of Zappos' top-notch customer care. One of Tony's friends wanted to challenge the customer service department to see if the employees were truly committed to making customers happy. After a night of barhopping, she and her friends (including Tony) returned to their hotel hungry. Since the hotel's room service was not available, they decided to see if Zappos could help them get a pizza delivered. The customer service rep that was working at that time did the research and found pizzerias near the hotel that were still open and would deliver at that time of the night. That employee didn't know that Tony was part of the group testing him. This story has been circulated and retold in so many places that it reinforces Zappos' customer service legends and contributes to its bottom line. Tony tells this story himself because it's a good example of "empowering your employees to do what's right for your brand, no matter how unusual or bizarre the situation."

In fact Tony was able to sell Zappos, a company built on a culture of customer service, to Amazon for an all-stock transaction valued at $1.2 billion.

PLAYBOOK IDEAS: HOW CAN YOU APPLY THIS TO YOUR ORGANIZATION?

1. As a leader of your company, how are you expanding your emotional intelligence and putting it into practice with customers and employees?

2. What is the "why" of your company? What aspects of who you are and what you represent are customers or employees most likely to identify with?

3. Call four clients and talk to them about what value your company has brought to them. Is it just about the features and benefits of the product/service you offer? Or is it more about quality interaction, caring, good communication, responsiveness, listening, flexibility, stress reduction, trustworthiness, respect, or positivity? What is the impact of the value you've given? Helping customers to think about what has really changed because of the value you've brought helps to deepen their appreciation of your company. You can use this information to develop new marketing messages.

4. Choose two recent customer interactions or engagements—one that went well and one that didn't. Along with your staff, go through the piggy bank exercise of putting a dollar coin in for every positive point of connection and taking six dollar coins out for every negative point of connection. See how many dollars or debits get collected for each. Are there any more coins that can still be deposited into the piggy bank of customer loyalty for the interaction/engagement that went awry?

5. Look at your direct competitors. What POCs do you do well that give you a competitive advantage? What are your competitors' POCs? How can you find out more about them and make sure your POCs are of higher value to the clients, more numerous, and more long lasting?

Additional supportive material and opportunities for growth can be found at www.customerloyaltyplaybook.com

CHAPTER 10
CUSTOMER SERVICE
STANDARDS CHART

When customers buy from you they want two things: (1) a quality product or service that is worth the price they are paying; (2) a great customer experience that is also worth the price they are paying. To have a truly outstanding company you need to provide both. One without the other won't make it in today's competitive world. The truth is that many vendors supply quality products and services. But companies that also provide a great customer experience stand out and often gain a competitive advantage. Customers want to be considered special, to get attention, to feel unique and valued, and to feel that you have empathy for their needs at every point of the buying experience. By engineering all the points of connection from your customer's point of view, your business will have the opportunity to offer what your customers really want.

Whether it's delivering a quality product or service or providing attentive customer service, it's all about mapping out and engineering a game-winning strategy. Lawyers have internal processes for handling client matters. Certified Public Accountants establish procedures for their financial data collection and reporting work. Manufacturers establish the process by which their product is assembled or mixed. Technology companies develop standard methods for troubleshooting problems in order to provide consistent service to their clients, no matter which technician shows up on site.

All these companies map out and engineer a process. How does your company engineer the customer experience? And according to what standard of service? I can check in to a low-end motel and get an adequate room without a lot of customer service--no one to help with my bags and a person behind the reception desk that disappears as soon as the transaction is done. Or, I can go into a Ritz Carlton and have my every need anticipated, so that I'm delighted and treated like royalty. Some people who have only experienced the low-end motel might think that's perfectly fine. Those who experience the Ritz Carlton on a regular basis would consider the low-end experience totally unacceptable. Now, think about your employees. Do they understand and handle customer service in the same manner? No, it depends on what they've previously experienced to define what they think is OK and what is not. If they've never experienced exemplary customer service, they may not know how to provide it. That's why you, as the business owner, need to establish standards in customer service and engineer those standards with great detail.

The Customer Service Standards Chart helps your company focus on the customer experience from their vantage point. This is like the chalkboard where you draw your game plan. Through its utilization, you will establish what your brand stands for and the kind of service you want your team to provide. As you delegate responsibilities and empower your staff through distributed leadership, they will pick up the ball and run with it even more than you could anticipate.

We previously talked about POC (point of connection). Every interaction you, your team, or your brand has with a customer is a point of connection, whether on the telephone, in an email, or in person. Other POCs would include marketing messages, the look and feel of your store or office, your company's website, and your product's design and packaging. Anything their five senses can pick up contributes to their customer experience. To engineer that, you plan and employ *operational standards* (how you conduct business) and *experiential standards* (how you treat your customers). You even explore what would "wow" them. You then anticipate what might go wrong, which we call a *service defect*. Finally, you plan what you will do to restore a good customer experience, which we call *service recovery*. Keep in mind that if your staff plans the customer experience themselves (often with the aid of a trained customer service facilitator), they are much more likely to implement the plan they've developed.

Planning is only the first step; execution is the key to obtaining the payoff. What is the payoff? The customers are delighted. They return again and again, yielding additional profits, predictable cash flow, and word of mouth referrals. Your staff bonds because they've worked out these standards together. They become proud of what they have accomplished, establish stronger connections with customers and each other, increase revenues for their departments, and gain greater appreciation of the good service provided by your suppliers or partners. They also develop a better understanding of your brand since they have taken actions that define your brand.

EIGHT STEPS TO ENGINEERING THE CUSTOMER EXPERIENCE

Use the Customer Service Standards Chart to engineer and improve your relationship with customers.

Step 1. Chunk all the POCs that your staff has with customers, There are marketing POCs, sales POCs, product POCs, and service POCs, to name a few. You may have other categories. Many times these POCs correlate to the departments in your company and that's good because you want to make the employees in those departments responsible for the POCs they have with customers.

Step 2. Define, step by step, the process of customer service interactions from beginning to end. For example, a couple comes into

Customer Service Standards Chart

Process *Restaurant Visit*   Stage of the Process *Pre-meal*

POC	Operational Standard	Experiential Standard	WOW! Moments	Service Defects	Service Recovery
Deliver menus	Hand each person an open menu right side up.	Smile, look at each person's face, be genuinely interested and caring.	Look for something to genuinely compliment them on, what they are wearing or how they occur to you. Offer a lighted magnifier.	The guest can't read English. Wrong pages inside the menu.	Get Victor who speaks 5 languages. Bring a new menu. Check all menus. LTAT (listen, thank, apologize, take action)

a restaurant, gets greeted and seated by a hostess, the waiter takes a drink order, delivers the drinks, takes a dinner order, delivers the courses of the dinner, delivers a check, processes payment, and the couple leaves. How are your customers handled step by step?

Step 3. Using this process, make a list of all the interactions and POCs that a particular department (or group of employees) has. Include everything you can: the look of the room, entrance, and the parking lot; greeting; initial conversation with customers; second conversation; emails; actions; and what the client might see, touch, smell, hear, or taste. Review the list and write down the POCs that stand out for you now. It may help to break down this process into stages so it's more manageable. Rome wasn't built in a day, so realize that you will engineer all your processes over time.

Step 4. Look at each POC. What is the operational standard used to create the quality you want to deliver? Example: Giving each customer a menu by handing it to him right side up.

Step 5. Look at each POC again and note the experiential standard used for each. What will ensure the customer experience that you want to deliver? Examples: Establishing eye contact; smiling; greeting personably.

Step 6. Define the "wow" moments that are possible for this POC. What are some wonderful or unexpected things that could be done or said to delight the client and anticipate his needs? Examples: Offering a lighted magnifying glass to someone in a dark restaurant; giving a heartfelt compliment.

Step 7. Identify possible service defects. What could possibly go wrong? Examples: The customer doesn't speak/read English; the menu has the wrong pages inside.

Step 8. Identify service recovery options. How can you rectify a service defect and restore a sense of trust? How can you show the client that you are committed to his delight in spite of a mistake? Examples: Listen to a problem, apologize, and then thank the person for bringing the problem to your attention. Check all the menus prior to meal service. Designate a member of your staff who is multilingual to assist a foreign client and ensure her needs are properly met.

By using this chart, you can engineer how the customer experiences the product/service you provide. There is much you can do to ensure that your customer feels well taken care of—even surprised and delighted—by giving much more than expected.

CASE STUDY

Imagine you and your family are visiting Disneyland. You've been riding rides, waiting on lines, seeing exhibits, meeting characters, walking, and seeing shows. The evening fireworks are over and you're leaving the park. You're tired and your kids are tired and cranky. You turn to your spouse and ask what parking lot you're in. She says she wrote it down but she's looked through everything and can't find it. Neither of you knows where to go. The kids are now fighting, which they always do when things are going downhill. So you walk toward an exit, talk to the parking lot attendants, and tell them you don't remember where you parked.

The parking lot staff has already anticipated this potential problem, however. They know that the final memory of the day is the one that makes the longest lasting impression. Disneyland is all about experiencing fun and magic, not the hassle of getting in and out of the park (or parking lot). So they developed a system to address this situation. When people arrive by car, they are parked according to the time of the day they enter the lot. Each row of cars is matched to the time when that row fills. Since people are eager to enter Disneyland and enjoy the fun, they often neglect to jot down their parking location or lose that information during a busy day of fun activities.

At the end of the day, when you're tired and ready to leave, but forget where you parked your car, the parking lot staff is ready. They ask you the time you arrived that day. They then drive you and your family by golf cart directly to the row that filled at that time, even if it's in a parking lot on the other side of the park. They've got it to a science so they can take you pretty much right to your car, not just the row. So your last experience at Disneyland is now one of the best experiences of the whole day.

Did a high level manager work out this system and tell the parking lot staff what to do? No. The staff saw the problem, knew it was not the right way for customers to end the day, created their own solution, and executed it. That's distributed leadership at work at its best, making the customer experience happen according to experiential standards, by anticipating the service defects and creating service recovery.

PLAYBOOK IDEAS: HOW CAN YOU APPLY THIS TO YOUR ORGANIZATION?

1. How do members of your staff like to be treated when they are the customers visiting another business? What POCs make the most difference for each of them?
2. How do customers react when you connect with them versus when you don't connect with them?
3. What are some examples of "wow" customer service that have happened at your company?
4. Why are some examples of service defects your company has experienced?
5. What service recovery techniques have you used?

6. How can you create a customer service standard chart for each of the processes in your business?
7. How do you prioritize which process to map out first?
8. Who would be on the customer service team for that process or POC? Who is the team leader or playmaker? By when would that POC or process design get done?
9. Will you create a plan to map out all your processes over the next year or two?
10. How are people held accountable to adhering to company standards?
11. What procedures can you put in place so everyone in your company meets these POC standards? (Some companies and teams have daily huddles to ensure that everyone is implementing the same game plan.)
12. Are there changes in your culture that might occur because of implementing these procedures?
13. What changes in culture can you execute now to improve POC standards? How/when/who will make them happen?
14. How will your POC chart change as changes occur in your business or business environment? How often will you review and update your game plans?

Additional supportive material and opportunities for growth can be found at www.customerloyaltyplaybook.com

CHAPTER 11
THE INNOVATION GROWTH CUBE

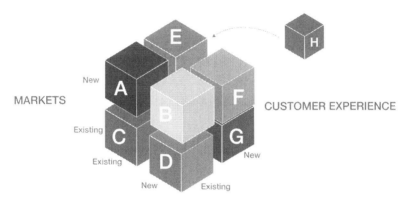

In this section we'll be addressing the growth of customer loyalty as it relates to choosing, acquiring, and retaining your ideal customer through targeted marketing, product/service expansion, and service growth strategies. In order to bring this into real world perspective, let's look at it from within the realm of overall business planning.

It is much easier to earn your customer's loyalty and to engage your employees when your strategies are clear, focused, and well communicated, and when both employees and clients can see themselves in your messages. Any sports coach goes for clarity so that all the players understand the game plan and its potential impact. If your marketing is not clear, you will fail to attract and keep your customer's attention, and your company's day-to-day existence will be like the mythological Greek king Sisyphus continuously pushing a boulder up a hill.

As you're planning your company's financial and business development goals from year to year, you have three choices of how you can expand and grow, as depicted in the growth cube above:

1. You can expand into new markets or more fully penetrate your existing markets (vertical axis).
2. You can expand the products/services you offer or continue to offer the same ones (horizontal axis).
3. You can expand and deepen the customer experience you provide by taking it to a whole new level of point of connection or you can continue to do business as you currently do (the depth axis).

In the growth strategy #1 continuum you are deciding who will be your targeted buyers. You may already be targeting a big enough segment and feel there is a lot more business to be had right where you are. Or, you may decide to go after a new segment in a different geographic area or a different group of prospects with the same or different needs. Examples of new markets: expanding your software for accountants into the legal market; marketing your retail-distributed barbecue sauce to wholesalers; offering your energy products in New Jersey as well as New York.

In the growth strategy #2 continuum you choose to continue to offer the same products and services you now offer. Or, you choose to innovate with new products or services. Examples of new products/services: developing a new phone app; bundling several existing products into a high value themed package; offering a highly spicy version of your barbecue sauce; introducing a new service that your clients have been asking for.

In the growth strategy #3 continuum you choose to keep the customer service experience the same or focus on taking it to a whole new level. Examples of new customer experiences: using customer relationship management software; using POC charts for all processes;

offering incentives to employees for over-the-top customer service reported by customers; developing management policies that focus on growing the culture of delighting customers; surveying clients on customer experience outcomes.

Great companies plan how they grow and strategize a game plan. They get everyone's input, choose one of the three growth strategies to be their primary strategic initiative, and then move forward to implement it. Not-so-great companies don't plan, don't seek input, and don't keep everyone informed. They leave too much to chance and wind up standing still.

How will you and your team decide where to innovate? You can make choices about expansion and growth based on the opportunities (or obstacles) you see and the resources (internal and external) you can utilize. This is called a SLOT analysis. Alone or together with your business planning team, list all the **S**trengths and **L**imitations of your company, including your company's capabilities and weaknesses. All things on this list are *internal* to your company. Next, create a list of *external* **O**pportunities available to your business in the world or your marketplace. Also list the **T**hreats—external events that could sabotage your business, such as regulations, tax laws, economic conditions, or new competitive pressures. As part of your research you can also examine parallel industries that offer interesting ideas to modify for your own situation. You might ask your best customers about their needs today and in the future, and how you can improve or adapt to their changing needs.

Through the practice of applying your list of strengths and limitations to the list of opportunities and threats, it starts to become apparent what the next and most effective growth strategy should be. It soon becomes clear if it is best to focus your resources on the target market (#1 above), the product or service (#2 above), or the customer experience (#3 above). Realistically, resources (time, people, money, mental energy) might only allow you to implement well one or two strategic initiatives per year, and probably not simultaneously.

In the last chapter we discussed designing a great customer experience and encouraged you to create POC charts for all your processes. Now, as we look at the big picture, which includes other elements of your business, we see how the customer experience fits in with targeted marketing and product/service offerings to create overall growth strategies.

Since customer loyalty increases sales and reduces costs, make sure any new initiative taken creates customer loyalty in any new market or with any new product/service offering. Choose well so that the customer experience is maximized and optimized in the rollout of these new initiatives.

Let's look at the eight sections (labeled A through H) of the growth cube to better understand what will be required in making a growth strategy selection for your game plan:

1. A = Developing a new market for an existing product using an existing customer experience design
2. B = Developing a new market for a new product using an existing customer experience design
3. C = Penetrating an existing market with an existing product using an existing customer experience design
4. D = Penetrating an existing market with a new product using an existing customer experience design
5. E = Developing a new market for an existing product while building an enhanced customer experience design
6. F = Developing a new market for a new product while building an enhanced customer experience design
7. G = Penetrating an existing market with a new product while building an enhanced customer experience design
8. H = Penetrating an existing market with an existing product while building an enhanced customer experience design

It may seems confusing until you choose one—A, B, C, D, E, F, G, or H. Then you can begin defining the three elements (target market, product or service, customer experience) for your business. I encourage you to get your team's input on where you are right now and where it's best to be headed as indicated in your SLOT analysis.

CASE STUDY

There is an online company that specializes in distributing period clothing from the 1950s—poodle skirts, retro dresses, and all kinds of accessories. They sell to schools and theater groups that put on shows set in the '50s like *Grease* and *Bye, Bye Birdie*. They also sell to people going to '50s dress-up parties and reunions. They were barely making a profit and had to turn the business around in order to keep it going. Over two years, they put several strategies in place:

> **Products.** They sold off old inventory and replaced it with '50s-style apparel that was more in demand for current buyers. They only invested in inventory that they knew would sell and, therefore, greatly increased their inventory turns. They examined their shipping needs and started using the best and most economical shipping for each size package and destination.

> **Target Markets.** They focused on penetrating current markets with new marketing strategies, updating their website and ordering system, increasing the use of social media, using pictures of models wearing the clothes instead of just pictures of clothing, and more blogging activity.

Customer Experience. They developed a strategy to regularly check-in with clients by phone about their customer service needs and wants. They created a service to provide online advertising (through social media) for the shows in which their customers were performing. They replaced their existing "after hours" answering service with one more aligned with their business needs and goals, which saved them money in the process. They began tracking incoming calls and created Point of Connection talking points for handling these calls and "wowing" their customers.

In addition, an employee with weak customer service skills was replaced by another with excellent abilities. A training program was created for this new hire, which is now used for all new hires.

The company's owner became better at empowering the employees to make their own decisions. This resulted in improved customer service and allowed the owner to become more involved with customers and in strategic planning.

The company has become much more profitable and the owner now takes a larger salary. She also has more time to take classes and acts as a mentor to other small business owners in her community.

PLAYBOOK IDEAS: HOW CAN YOU APPLY THIS TO YOUR ORGANIZATION?

1. Lead your team through a SLOT analysis. For more objective results, you might want to hire a trained facilitator to lead your team through the process. Conduct your market and industry research and your customer and employee assessments first so you have the information at hand.

2. Decide if you are going to invest in a customer experience initiative, a new target market, or a new product or service offering. Select A, B, C, D, E, F, G or H. Formulate your game plan. It is preferable to implement your initiatives one at a time, otherwise you risk becoming overwhelmed, confused, or short on resources, and accomplish nothing.

3. Pinpoint when, how, and who (the playmaker) will execute these initiatives. This becomes your strategic growth plan.

4. After determining some overall 12-18 month general initiatives, chunk the execution into 90-day plans. What specific measurable goals will your company accomplish during each 90-day period? Who will execute the plans? What monthly milestones must be achieved in order to meet your goals by the end of each 90-day period?

5. Communicate these initiatives clearly to your employees and get their buy-in on the 90-day plans and the monthly milestones. Ask for their input and ideas. Have a rollout party that your employees plan. Make it fun.

Additional supportive material and opportunities for growth can be found at www.customerloyaltyplaybook.com

CHAPTER 12
TARGET MARKET PRODUCT MATRIX

Target Market Product Matrix

Start/End Date:_____

PRODUCTS	%	TARGET MARKETS				
		1	2	3	4	5
A						
B						
C						
D						
E						
F						
G						
H						
I						
J						
	100%					

At this point, we are going to focus on two of the three aspects of revenue generation and developing client loyalty: target markets and product/service offerings. The more ideal these become, the more your total strategy and game plan will flourish.

Ideal clients have a need and know that your company can meet their needs. They find great value in your product or service. They pay on time. You enjoy working with them and they enjoy working with you. They refer new business to you. They understand your value proposition and become loyal raving fans. Wouldn't it be lovely if *all* your clients were just like that?

Ideal products and services provide great value to the ideal target market, because the offerings meet or exceed the needs of your clients. You can create systems around these products and services so you can replicate them consistently and produce them excellently over and over again. Your costs, therefore, decrease with less rework and greater systemization and speed. Your products and services inspire your team's creativity, making them enthusiastic about improving the products and services in response to changing client demands.

Think these ideas are just a dream? They don't have to be.

The Target Market Product Matrix is a tool that helps businesses focus on generating revenues through the matching of ideal clients to ideal offerings. It creates revenue projections that can be part of your business plan. It builds the target market/product infrastructure that builds trust among your loyal clients.

The most important decision for any business owner or executive team to make is determining the company's target market. The second most important decision is determining what monetized products or services fulfill the needs of that target market. Once these decisions are made, sales revenue projections can be determined.

The Target Market Product Matrix is a model that streamlines this process and provides clarity. In my experience, many small and midsize businesses create products and services, offer them to a general audience, and hope that something lands. Using this matrix forces businesses to have an intentional strategy and points out how ineffective, nebulous, and vague those unsuccessful strategies have been in the past. Confusing game plans don't win games.

OVERVIEW OF THE TARGET MARKET PRODUCT MATRIX

Using the matrix is a multi-step building process. Here is the overview of how the matrix can be useful in creating income projections for your game plan:

- Enter the target markets for your business across the top of the matrix (items 1-5).
- Enter the products/services you plan to offer down the left column of the matrix (items A-J).
- Use the six-step process below to allocate the percentage of your revenue that will be coming from a specific product sold to a specific target market

By using this matrix you can then take each percentage and multiply it by the amount of gross revenue you want to generate to determine how much revenue will come from that target market's purchase of that offering. You can use those figures for your income projections.

Before we get into the six-step process, let's take a close look at target markets and products and services.

DETERMINING AND UNDERSTANDING TARGET MARKETS

What are your target markets? Perhaps you produce barbeque sauce. You might sell your product to supermarkets for resale, to restaurants for meal preparation, and to consumers through your website. You would then have three target markets.

Your target market is who you sell to. It is a subset of the general market that has specific needs and wants that your product or service satisfies. The narrower the target the better since specialized markets have specific needs that you can directly address. You determine your target markets through research. Who has a need? Is the market big enough for you to generate a profit? How long will this need last? Are there a lot of competitors? Is there a need in the market everyone else has missed?

It is imperative that you and your team thoroughly understand each of your target markets. In order to do so, you will want to find out everything you can about each market's demographics, psychographics, buying habits, lifestyle, the words they use and respond to, and where/how they can be reached. Just like a coach studies his players and the opposition's players, the more you know, the better the decisions you make.

Demographics. What are the statistical characteristics of your target market? Can this market be segmented into subgroups? Research information on age, gender, ethnicity, education, socio-economic level, geographic location, marital status, number of children, net-worth, home ownership status, or other facts relevant to your industry and product/service. For instance, if you sell pet supplies, it's important for you to define this consumer as a pet owner. If you are a marketing consultant, you may want to pinpoint people who have "marketing" in their job title or position description. If your business sells to other businesses, you'll want to gather information about the business, including who does the purchasing for that business.

Psychographics. What attitudes, values, needs, and fears does your target customer or client have? What questions might he ask? What problem does he have that your product/ service can solve? What are the issues in his life that cause this problem? What's limiting him? What does he prioritize in his life? What makes him happy? What are his long and short-term goals? What's his vision for his life? What will he lose if he doesn't get this need satisfied? Is he politically liberal or conservative? Adventurous or risk-averse? Local or global in perspective? Strongly committed or mildly interested?

Buying habits. Does your target customer or client buy your product/service often? Does he buy something similar or related? How much money does he spend? What does he prioritize in his purchasing? How much research does he do before making a purchase? Whose opinion/feedback matters to him? What is his internal state of mind when he makes a purchase? When does he buy your type of product? Does he buy your product/service online, at a department store, at a specialty store, or at an office? How does he define value? What would he usually pay for your type of product/service? What would he value more if you wanted to offer more value for a higher price? How does he view you compared to your competitors? Does he have needs not being served by your competitors?

Lifestyle. Describe your ideal client's typical day from the moment he gets up to the moment he goes to bed. How does the day start? What are the interactions at home? How does the workday go? Does he take a lunch or eat at his desk? How long is the workday? What happens after work? How does he spend his weekends? Who are the important people in his life? What shapes his decisions? How does he relax? What hobbies and interests does he have? How can knowing his lifestyle patterns make your offerings more valuable or make him more accessible to your messages?

Words used by your target customer. He needs to see himself inside your messages. Are you using the words he would use and completely relate to? What search words does he use online and are these reflected in your written and verbal messages? Are you using those words and phrases on your website, in your networking, and in your brochures and promotional materials? What ads (yours or your competitors) does he respond to best?

Reaching your target customer. Where does he hang out? What magazines, TV shows, radio shows, websites, newspapers, movies, and books does he read/watch/listen to? What events does he attend? Who could refer your company to him? Who are his trusted advisors? Does he go to industry conferences, conduct business on the golf course, have mutual contacts, or belong to social media groups? Does he network with others? Does he network regularly through organized referral groups, social media groups, service organizations, sport events, or non-profit events?

How do you obtain this information? Some of it might be collected in industry research available at your public library's business reference section. Libraries purchase licenses to databases that contain information about individual consumers, consumer groups, individual businesses, and industries. Many of these databases can be accessed on-site on library computers and are free to everyone. A reference librarian can help you find information. Bring a flash drive to download information or email it to yourself.

The library is also a good source for learning some things about the business environment of your target market. Are there anticipated regulations or material shortages that will hamper him? Is his technology old? You can find out how big the market is and who the other players are. Your decision on the viability of a target market will be influenced by how many competitors are slicing up the market and if those competitors are strong or weak.

Most of the lifestyle and psychographic information will come from your clients or from focus groups you conduct or events you sponsor where you actually talk to customers and prospects. Developing an online survey, while helpful, won't fully provide you with the necessary stories around your data to help you with marketing messages. You will want to hear and record the words that your potential customers use to describe their needs. Using their language in your marketing messages will resonate with them, building trust and empathy.

For information within or about your industry, take other business people out to lunch to gain their insights and views, read trade magazines, visit industry association websites, and talk with other vendors in your field.

Collecting data and understanding more about your target markets will allow you to:

1. Create products/services that better address their needs and problems
2. Draft messages that ideal clients will find irresistible
3. Put these messages in the places and in the form your prospects will see
4. Create effective calls-to-action so that prospects will contact you
5. Attract referral agents that will send you ideal clients

When you have decided on your target markets, write them across the top of this matrix in the boxes 1-5. Having one or two target markets is preferable to having 3, 4, or 5, because your efforts and resources will be less diluted. I've provided 5 columns so you can do some "what-if" planning. But I highly recommend you focus most of your resources on your top two.

DETERMINING YOUR PRODUCTS AND SERVICES

In essence, the products and services you develop and sell are the *solutions* you offer your clients. For example, if you manufacture barbecue sauce you might sell it in several ways. You can offer it by the jar directly to consumers through your website or through retailers. You can sell it in a package with an apron or other BBQ-related products. You can offer it by the case with minimal labeling for purchase by a restaurant. You can even offer it with a customized label so that a restaurant can sell it under its own name to its regular customers for home use. These are four different products that go on lines A, B, C, and D on the matrix.

Perhaps you have many different products and prefer to think in terms of product lines. Or, if you have different departments for each product or service you offer, you can group your products/services any way that makes sense for your company's structure.

If you offer services, such as accounting, legal, or web design services, these can be listed separately according to how you package them. For example, you would place hourly billing, retainer contracts, annual service contracts, and passive income products on separate lines.

When you have determined your products or product groups, list them in the boxes marked A to J.

SIX STEPS TO REVENUE PLANNING

The next six steps help you focus on building a revenue plan and financial projections for your company.

1. Determine the period of time in which you will sell your product/service to each target market in the matrix. Are you planning for the next six, twelve, or eighteen months? Write the start date and end date on the line in the upper right hand corner.

2. Not every product is geared to every market. Look at each box in the matrix and place a small x inside the box where you plan to sell that product to that target market.

3. Now focus on the % column next to boxes A-J. Write in the % of your revenue you would like that product/service or product grouping to generate. Make sure it adds up to 100%.

4. Look at the percentage you just wrote next to Product A. Distribute that percentage horizontally into the boxes where you put small x's. If the percentage is 10% and there are 2 small x's under your two target markets where that product will be sold, will those target markets be responsible for 5% each or 3% and 7%? Repeat for each row.

5. Evaluate the income plan you've made. Consider what you've done so far as your first draft. Do you like your distribution? Can it be properly executed? What resources might be needed? Is it realistic to have that many products going to that many target markets? What products/services are you looking to grow most, revenue-wise? Are there items, product lines, or services that don't generate enough profit and can be eliminated? This is the step where you build a better future for your company by targeting more ideal customers with more ideal products and services. You can add in line items or target markets that present opportunities. Look over your SLOT analysis that we discussed in the last chapter. What is going on in each of your target market's industries that will affect their purchases from you? What's happening with your competitors that will affect your planning? What were last year's revenues? Are you content with sustaining or incrementally increasing last year's figures or are you looking for larger gains? If you're looking to increase revenue, which areas might provide the best opportunity for growth? This is where you get to proactively plan how you will seize your future instead of just accepting what comes your way. You can look at this step as "what if" planning. *What if* we used these numbers? *What if* we cut this out? *What if*

we added this? This is where you make choices and create clarity and focus. You may wind up creating several versions of this matrix, testing different scenarios before you make a decision to go forward. This is a critical part of your playbook. It's where you make decisions about putting in the defense or the offense; it's where you adapt the strategy because of playing conditions. It's where you create new plays because of current situations and resources.

6. Multiply the percentages from each target market/product cell by the revenue desired. For example, if you want to achieve revenues of $5 million next year from sales of your barbecue sauce and you want 20% of that revenue to come from sales to restaurants, then $1 million will come from restaurant sales. Now you have a target. You can then design the marketing tactics, sales strategies, team development, and operational structures to allow you to reach that goal.

HAVE SOME FUN WITH YOUR CLIENT AVATAR

Understanding your target client is the most important thing you can do in your business. I recommend you take on the following exercise, get your staff involved, and include some fun while you invite your client avatar to all your meetings.

What is a client avatar? An avatar is a fictitious character created by combining the common aspects of your most ideal clients. It could be based on an end user (B2C) or the business owner/purchasing agent/department head (B2B). Give this ideal customer a name and circulate this information throughout your company. Write up all your research about him in a profile and make sure everybody reads it. Discuss him and his needs in your staff meetings. Put relevant aspects up on your website and in other marketing materials so clients who share the same profile know that you are talking directly to them. When your avatar is regularly discussed and the plans that you execute constantly revolve around serving your avatar, your company will have achieved the status of being customer-focused.

Suppose your avatar is named Priscilla. In your meetings, save a seat for Priscilla. Ask questions such as: What does Priscilla think about this idea? What value does Priscilla get from what you just proposed? Where does Priscilla network? Where can we find her? What does Priscilla see on our website that catches her eye and makes her want to read more? Who is talking with Priscilla that will refer her to us?

CASE STUDY

Jennifer is a lawyer with a growing practice. She and her associates are litigators handling a variety of claims. They have several dream clients who give them steady and plentiful work. They also have several demanding clients that also give them business. The challenge is that Jennifer and her associates must show up at court at irregular times all over the state. They also have to be responsive to email notices. Some of the more demanding clients are unreasonable in their requests. Since the lawyers' schedules are changing daily, it has become difficult for anyone to plan a personal life. They are also getting burned out by this work. They have interests they'd like to pursue with small businesses, but that has been placed on the back burner since the litigation cases are currently paying the bills and many of these cases will take months to resolve.

Jennifer and her team used the matrix tool to map out how they will gradually reduce their reliance on litigation cases and gradually increase their work with small business owners. They put together a two-year plan that takes the percentages from 90% litigation/10% small business to 50%/50% and then to 30%/70%. Once they had agreed on these targets, they then devised strategies to move some of the more demanding litigation clients to other attorneys. They had also decided not to take on new litigation cases from new clients, to attract more small business work, and to generally plan a business that was more aligned with the work they wanted to do and with the lifestyle they wanted to live.

Energy picked up at the firm as Jennifer and her associates could see a brighter future being shaped. They all bought into the gradual nature of the transition so that they could guarantee revenue levels and everyone's employment. The litigation business was handled better since it was now in transition. Everyone at the firm earnestly pursued opportunities to seek small business clients.

These plans worked. Not only has the firm maintained its revenue levels, but it is also on course to attract more work in the small business arena.

PLAYBOOK IDEAS: HOW CAN YOU APPLY THIS TO YOUR ORGANIZATION?

1. Prepare a SLOT analysis as described in the last chapter. Get agreement on your target market/product mix and share it with your whole team so that everyone knows the directions you're taking.
2. How can the Target Market Product Matrix be helpful to your marketing department (in-house or outsourced)?
3. How can the matrix be helpful to your product/service development team?
4. What input could your customer service team give about the way these numbers affect their work?
5. Using your 90-day execution plans (mentioned in the last chapter), what activities can be implemented so your plans actually get executed?

6. What new developments or opportunities could come along and change these targets? What distractions might arise that you can ignore?

7. Who on your team is committed to meeting these goals? Do you have a commitment from your team to proactively accomplish each and every number? Have any playmakers/champions come forth that will hold each of your teams accountable?

8. Do you have a reporting mechanism you can use—e.g., a very visual scoreboard, chart or dashboard—so that the whole team can see and know when you are accomplishing milestones that lead up to the targets?

9. How can you make these milestones and targets real for each employee?

10. Do you have an ideal client avatar? What is your avatar's name? Is this "client" referred to in all your marketing meetings? What impact has this had in turning your company from a business-centric organization to a client-centric organization?

Additional supportive material and opportunities for growth can be found at www.customerloyaltyplaybook.com

CHAPTER 13
MARKETING SPIDER WEB

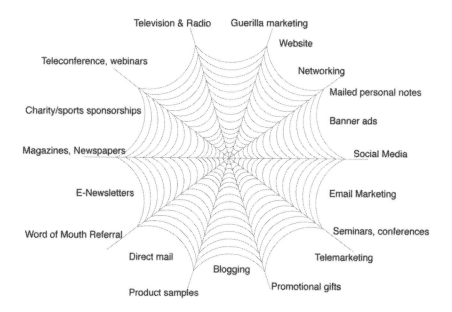

Television & Radio Guerilla marketing

Website

Teleconference, webinars

Networking

Mailed personal notes

Charity/sports sponsorships

Banner ads

Magazines, Newspapers

Social Media

E-Newsletters

Email Marketing

Word of Mouth Referral

Seminars, conferences

Direct mail

Telemarketing

Blogging

Product samples

Promotional gifts

If you draw a large circle and then put about twenty markers on the circumference of the circle as noted, you can create a marketing spider web. In nature, the purpose of a spider web is to catch and keep flies. It's sticky and has an interlocking matrix that keeps flies from escaping. The same is true of a marketing spider web. You want to catch a prospect and keep him bouncing from one marketing touchpoint to another so that he thinks your company is everywhere and at the top of your industry. The more the prospect sees your company touted for its expertise, leading an industry initiative, or playing an active role in its field, the more he becomes convinced of your competitive advantage and that you are the one to choose if he needs your product or service. The longer the prospect is caught in the web, the more likely he is to eventually make a purchase. In fact, research shows that a purchaser's likelihood of buying grows significantly after eight touchpoints.

Each of the twenty markers becomes a potential entry point onto your web. A customer or client may enter through your website or blog, a word-of-mouth referral, a direct mail piece, a networking event, a webinar or teleclass, an event that your company sponsors, traditional radio or TV advertising, a social media site, a magazine or newspaper, or a host of other potential marketing activities. This is not to say your company needs to do them all. You'd be better off focusing on 4-6 tactics and doing them well.

However, there is a key component in any marketing activity you choose to do. Each one needs to have a Call-to-Action (CTA), which sends the prospect to another point on the marketing web. If someone enters your web through a referral, she might head to your website. Your CTA on the website might be a white paper that she signs up to receive. The CTA she sees in the white paper might advertise the teleseminar you are conducting. She then attends the teleseminar, so you send a follow-up thank you note via email or snail mail. The CTA from the thank you note directs her to your blog, which then directs her to your YouTube channel. From there she can connect with you on Facebook, Yelp, Twitter, or LinkedIn where she sees others recommending or commenting on your services. You get the idea. By this time, the prospects knows a lot about your company, your brand, your services, and your other clients who have needs similar to hers. If you provide a special offer, like a free consultation, she will likely take advantage of your offer because you've earned her trust over multiple informative and courteous interactions. Multiple connections through a variety of media have helped her develop an affinity for your company and your brand identity. Your strategic handoff is working, over and over again, keeping the ball in motion and moving down the field. It's a winning game strategy.

This method works extremely well if you keep the following four points in mind:

1. **Always have a clear message**

    What is your clear message about the people you serve, the problem you solve, and the outcome you promise? Repeat this message over and over again in all your marketing activities and networking. Use the same words to get started and then expand with stories, FAQs, and the "how" and "why" of your product/service. But always start with a clear message about the customers you serve, the problem they have, and the outcome you promise. Doing this makes your company recognizable, convincing, credible, and inviting to the person you're trying to attract. People love repetition---that is how they learn. It gives them certainty, which makes them feel secure. That's how Kleenex® got to be synonymous with tissues and Xerox® became synonymous with photocopying. Consistently using your logo and company colors also make your company and brand more recognizable.

    There are benefits to you as well. You can repurpose content, which cuts down on your company's overall work. If you conduct a seminar, you can have it videotaped and uploaded to your website or YouTube. You can have the content transcribed and edited into a document that can be downloaded from your website or distributed to article sites. You can also send it by mail or email to specific clients/prospects. You can use just the audio portion to create a podcast and post it to iTunes. The slides from your presentation can be posted on SlideShare. Links to all these items can be shared with your followers through various social media sites. Perhaps you can combine that content with other content to form a book. As you can see, there are many ways to repurpose content. And as that content becomes visible in multiple ways on the Internet, the search engines find it and increase its impact for you, giving you greater visibility.

Your message is even more effective if it is personal and authentic. Many companies' advertising is centered on a personality because people oriented stories resonate with potential buyers and are memorable and authentic. Authenticity means that it is real, from the heart, not overstated, and not vague. Authenticity is also closely linked to believability, which earns a client's trust and empathy. If your message is authentic, she can see herself in the message and feel that you and your company truly understand her needs. Therefore, she will trust the product or service solution your company is offering.

2. Address your ideal client

It can't be stressed enough. Knowing your target market is the key to attracting rather than chasing after your potential customers. In the last chapter, we addressed creating avatars (fictitious characters created by combining the common aspects of your most ideal clients). You will want to create an ideal client avatar for each of your target markets.

Now is the time to use all the knowledge you acquired about your ideal client avatar. You want your website, your brochures, your speeches and the words coming out of your mouth when networking to resonate so deeply with your ideal prospect that each prospect says, 'That's exactly what I was looking for. It's perfect. Where do I sign up?' Then you want her to go tell everyone else she knows with a similar need to search you out.

The best way to have that kind of impact is to use her words to start with. Those words have emotional associations for her. She chose them to express the 'pain' of her situation. They resonate with her. When you use them, she perceives that she's been listened to. So go talk to your ideal clients, record the actual words they use. Then incorporate them into your marketing messages.

When you can put yourself completely in the shoes of your ideal clients, they will feel that what you offer is exclusively created for them. They will then be drawn to you like moths to a flame. Your referrals will exponentially increase saving you marketing dollars. Your costs will go down since you know your market and offerings well and your systems are repeatable. You will become the "expert" in your niche and it will be tough for a competitor to make inroads. You can't know your ideal client too well. Understanding your target is the key part of your game plan.

People often ask, "If my ideal client profile is so targeted and narrow, won't that rule out a lot of other buyers?" The answer is that you will attract clients more readily if your message is targeted. This is your *intentional* market, the center of your bull's-eye. There will always be *accidental* buyers in the rings around the bulls-eye. You don't directly market to them but somehow they find you. Perhaps they were referred, or are mildly interested, or buy in small quantities to see if what you offer has value for them. This information from non-targeted, accidental buyers may induce you to expand into related markets. You will already have some data about which potential markets find value in your offerings. At that point you might want to establish a second target market—and avatar—for this expansion market.

3. Execute with high quality

People innately believe that how you do anything is how you do *everything*. If your company's marketing is sloppy or inconsistent, it may be perceived that your product/service will also be delivered that way. If your company's communications are intelligent, grammatically correct, and spell-checked, it shows that you will provide similarly professional services or products.

If customers have a negative marketing experience, it leaves a bad impression that is hard to overcome.

You want your company to establish the trust necessary to reduce the prospect's perceived risk if she were to make a purchase. That's why companies want their websites to be up to date, focused on client's needs, and professional. Your website—like all your other marketing tools—is the face of your business and often the first step in establishing brand trust. Make sure all your marketing activities show attention to detail. This reinforces to prospective clients that they will receive the same quality experience if they purchase from your business.

If your company is just starting out, you probably have a limited budget. Focus on getting one marketing activity done consistently with high quality. Once that is executed and shown to be effective, add a second activity and use a call-to-action (CTA) to magnify the effectiveness of both. Then add a third and a fourth marketing activity, perhaps by repurposing content. Be consistent and professional. Sacrificing quality is not an option.

4. Be informational, not "salesy"

Since we live in a digital age with a proliferation of information and tools like the Internet to help make choices, a salesperson that gives you a sales presentation immediately upon meeting you is now deemed offensive in most industries. It's like asking a person to marry you without going through a dating stage. Education-based marketing is about providing timely information to people, which draws them into your marketing spider web. If your marketing is too *salesy*, people will be repulsed and your efforts will be ineffective. Certainly, you are in business to make sales. If the customer senses that's your only agenda, you'll get nowhere. The customer is very much in charge and will choose to buy from your company when you have earned the right (and the trust) to sell to him. To earn that trust think of yourself as an assistant buyer, an advocate who helps him clarify what he wants and why, an industry expert who educates him on the industry's offerings and the associated benefits to him--a supporter who has his best interests in mind, even if it means not purchasing from you. Educating the client allows you to build a relationship so the customer/client feels he can trust your company, your brand, and your products/services.

CASE STUDY

Charles is a photographer who did not understand the concept of call-to-action. He owned a studio in a fairly affluent, well-educated community of culturally diverse families. He specialized in family portraits and children's photos. He did beautiful work and was great with kids. He was able to bring out their personalities and set up the lighting and environment so that the photos were striking and beautiful. He knew most families would prefer to patronize the services of a local photographer so he rented (for one-time use only) a list of names and address of a thousand families in his neighborhood. He then created and printed a postcard of beautiful photos to advertise his studio. He sent them out to this mailing list in plenty of time to attract some family portraits for the holiday season. Despite this hefty investment, he got zero responses.

When I spoke with Charles, I asked him to show me the postcard. The only information on it was his phone number. There was no special offer or other call-to-action to compel the recipients to contact him and no website listed so that those interested could check him out online and learn more about his services. If he had been aware of the marketing spider web, he could have added his website address and a special offer on the postcard that would entice potential customers to visit his website. Since these were families with young children whose parents were interested in quality education, he could have offered a free downloadable educational coloring book, perhaps of holiday outfits of different countries or ethnicities. He could have included his marketing message and sample photos in this coloring book. Those interested would have entered their email addresses to get the coloring books so that he could build a database of interested prospects, a subset of ideal clients from the more general list he rented. He also would then have had the ability to send them future newsletters, photography samples, or touched them in other ways until they actually bought a portrait package. Knowing that they were interested enough to register on his website, he could have invited them to an event, or a gallery or street fair where he was appearing. He could have had multiple calls-to-action if he had captured their information.

The coloring book could have helped him build his brand as a photographer who educates and cares about children. As a free offering, it differentiates him from a photographer who offers a coupon or an extra photo if a purchase is made. He would be viewed as someone who is generous and educational.

Instead, Charles missed all of these opportunities because the only call-to-action on the postcard was a phone number. He failed to understand that today's consumer prefers to check out a vendor's website prior to making a call or a purchase of any size or significance. He didn't know that most people don't make a purchase until they've seen a message eight times. He didn't leverage an opportunity to offer something in exchange for an email address and many future calls-to-action.

PLAYBOOK IDEAS: HOW CAN YOU APPLY THIS TO YOUR ORGANIZATION?

1. Does your company have a marketing spider web? If not, draw a circle and put in the entry points you currently employ.

2. At each entry point, list the specific calls-to-action you use to keep interested prospects continually moving around your marketing spider web, making it sticky for them.

3. Describe the last three marketing initiatives or activities your company did and the calls-to-action you used. What other calls-to-action could you have used? What will you incorporate in the future and put in your playbook?

4. Is each of the entry points you listed up-to-date and of high quality? Do they reflect your brand? Do you do 4-6 marketing activities really well . . . or in a half-hearted fashion?

5. Is each of your marketing entry points educational or salesy? If it's a mix of both, what is the ratio? Do you actively manage that ratio so you're not leaning too heavily on the salesy side? Many social media experts say only one out of ten should be self-promotional.

6. Have you identified your target market and created an ideal client avatar with a name and set of attributes? What's the name of the avatar that represents your ideal client? Can everyone in the organization recognize the name of your avatar, as well as describe her and her needs, her concerns, and the outcome she is looking for (rather than what you are selling)?

7. What is your main message? Is it clear and concise? Can everyone in your organization say it from memory? How does it relate to your target market? Are you incorporating words that your ideal clients have used with you? Do you use it in every marketing activity, spoken or written? Does everyone on your staff use it when speaking to their personal and professional contacts?

8. Does your marketing spider web reflect the habits of your target market? Discuss ten ways that your marketing spider web incorporates the habits and needs of your avatar.

Additional supportive material and opportunities for growth can be found at www.customerloyaltyplaybook.com

CHAPTER 14
PUTTING TOGETHER YOUR PLAYBOOK

A picture is worth a thousand words. Coaches use diagrams of plays to communicate in a way that words cannot. The image provides the concept. Words then expand the meaning and give details.

Have you put together your playbook? In football, the playbook is a collection of strategies that a coach uses to push his team forward to the end zone and achieve a win. In *The Customer Loyalty Playbook* there are a dozen strategies with multiple ways of using each to achieve a win in your business. I encourage you to write up each strategy that is appropriate for your company and put them into a notebook, either on paper or digitally. Make them the basis of your annual or quarterly planning process. Share them with your team. Use them to build your loyal customer/client base and achieve all the winning benefits, described in the 9 compelling reasons defined in Chapter 1.

You can put these nine compelling reasons on the first page of your playbook to keep them top-of-mind for each member of your team.

Customer loyalty is the game played by winning businesses because:

1. Loyal customers generate profit.
2. Loyal customers buy more.
3. Loyal customers give referrals.
4. Loyal clients are less price sensitive.
5. Loyal customers pay on time, which improves your cash flow.

6. Loyal customers who interact with an engaged staff generate an upward value spiral.
7. Loyal customers give your company a competitive advantage.
8. Loyal customers lead to reduced servicing costs.
9. Loyal customers are more forgiving.

Helpful resources for creating your own company playbook can be found at www.customerloyaltyplaybook.com. Make developing your company team more fun by including your employees in the selection of a team name, creating a team T-shirt or jersey, and choosing a team mascot. You can set up a scoreboard to help the team measure how close they are getting to the goals you've identified as "touchdowns."

Use this playbook regularly. Here are some other things to add to your playbook to reinforce the plays you've already selected:

Share this book with your staff. Make it available to everyone. Go to www.customerloyaltyplaybook.com to get a full-screen picture of each graphic. Print and distribute the graphics or project each one onto your wall or screen, and then lead a lively discussion on each picture. Look at the discussion questions at the end of each chapter or on the website. You might want to schedule a series of "lunch and learns" and cover one or two topics/pictures each time.

Examine your leadership. The most inspiring and powerful leaders are those who are authentic, open-minded, and empowering, and who listen to and value everyone else's contributions and opinions. Ask for feedback on your leadership style. Ask how you can be more supportive or a better leader. Get your managers to do the same with their subordinates. Do this examination one-on-one or in small groups. Earn respect and trust rather than demand it.

Work with a specialist or coach. Get help examining and developing yourself as a leader in your organization and in your life outside the organization. Your business will only grow as much as you grow as a leader. You may be hindering your growth through subconscious values and beliefs that limit you. Coaching can help you release those limiting values and beliefs and unleash amazing growth.

Train and develop your managers. Leadership begins at the top. Whether you implement a program in-house or send them to outside workshops, your managers will greatly benefit from training and development. These new soft skills and deepening awareness of emotional intelligence will help them become better supervisors and contribute to their growth as well as the growth of your business. It will also lead to greater job satisfaction for everyone.

Train and develop your employees. Let them know you care by investing in their skills and growth. Through training and development, your employees will gain more awareness of building customer loyalty and improving the customer experience, which in turn, will result in their ability to handle customers with ease and grace.

Create a culture committee. This task force can examine the culture with you and share everyone's ideas on what the company values really are. The committee can help plan worthwhile activities and celebrations, create rewards and incentives, and even develop a company blog that all employees can read or contribute to.

Develop an inventory of "wow" stories. Supportive relationships with customers—as well as among employees—result in positive stories. These stories reinforce the Point of Connection standards you've put into place, the values your company espouses, the ways in which staff have stepped up to show initiative and develop their leadership, and the results the clients get. Find ways to record these stories and share them as a company.

YOUR CHALLENGE

What will your company be like this time next year? How will your company's culture be different? How will your leadership be different?

Unlike football, the players in your business are on the field all the time, not just for four quarters in a two or three hour game. As such, your business game plan would benefit from an implementation strategy. I challenge you to select your top playbook strategy, assign a start date, and make things happen with your staff. If you just let the whirlwind of everyday operations consume all of your energy and focus, your company will stay stuck. Instead, take that first step to exercise your leadership to inspire your employees and move your company into the end zone to achieve your goals. Game winning strategies are abundant. Will you take the challenge to execute them?

RESOURCES

Additional Resources and authors where you can find out more information about customer loyalty and the leadership and infrastructure that earns it

Simon Sinek, *Start With Why, How Great Leaders Inspire Everyone to Take Action*

Michael Gerber, *Emyth Revisited, Why Most Small Businesses Don't Work and What to Do About It*

Patrick Lencioni, *Getting Naked, A Business Fable about Shedding the Three Fears that Sabotage Client Loyalty*

Liz Wiseman, *Multipliers, How the Best Leasers Make Everyone Smarter*

Byron Katie, *Loving What Is, Four Questions that can Change Your Life*

Carol Dweck, PH.D., *Mindset, The New Psychology of Success*

Daniel Pink, *Drive, the Surprising Truth About What Motivates Us*

Frederick Reichheld, *The Loyalty Effect, the Hidden Force Behind, Growth, Profits and Lasting Value*

Frederick Reichheld, *The Ultimate Question, How Net Promoter Companies Thrive in a Customer-Driven World*

Leonard Inghilleri, Micah Solomon, *Exceptional Service, Exceptional Profit, the Secrets of Building a Five-Star Customer Service Organization*

John R. DiJulius III, *What's the Secret? To Providing a World-Class Customer Experience*

Tony Hsieh, *Delivering Happiness, A Path to Profits, Passion, and Purpose*

Lee Cockerell, *Creating Magic, 10 Common Sense Leadership Strategies from a Life at Disney*

Edward M. Hallowell, *Shine: Using Brain Science to Get the Best from Your People*

ABOUT THE AUTHOR

Jeri Quinn is the President and founder of Driving Improved Results, an executive coaching and management consulting firm that supports CEO's of small and mid-size companies in creating customer-centric sales-driven cultures that generate client loyalty, engaged employees and bottom line results. With more than 30 years experience leading her own companies as well as coaching other business owners, she has developed experience in over 40 industries. Jeri is committed to empowering others to grow, learn, and play a big game. It is a theme running through her entire life as a teacher, dance/movement therapist, wife, mother, business owner, friend, coach, consultant, author and speaker. Jeri received her BA from Lycoming College and her MA in Dance Movement Therapy from New York University. She lives and works in both New York and Pennsylvania.

Coaching and Consulting:

Dynamic proven systems that grow you as a leader of next level companies

Specialist in generating customer/client loyalty and an engaged culture

Expert in professional development with leaders, managers, and teams

Keynote and Seminar Topics
Double Your Profit by Engaging Your Front Line
Forever Fans: How to Boost Customer Loyalty
Creating 'Wow!': Designing the Customer Experience
All presentations are customized to the wants and needs of the
audience.

Books:
This book can be ordered in large quantities for distribution
within a large company, association or convention. It can be customized to fit your needs and have a forward by your leader.
Watch for other business books from Jeri Quinn.

Products:
Concepts and game strategies in business books are only useful if
they are implemented. You will find inexpensive implementation
tools on our website.
Make sure to visit the website's Resource Center for free resources,
suggestions for further education on client loyalty, leadership,
professional development and business growth.

www.CustomerLoyaltyPlaybook.com
www.DrivingImprovedResults.com

Three reasons why you should coach and consult with Driving
Improved Results:
1. It's lonely at the top. You don't have to do this alone.

2. You can get results faster with coaching and consulting where
we will work together to bring greater profits to your bottom line,
create loyal customers that buy and refer more, and develop more
committed and productive employees.

3. Jeri's background in education and psychology gives her an advantage in communicating business and leadership concepts so that you implement. This is in contrast to others who have business experience but don't necessarily have the ability to lead you to execute in your own business.

If you'd like information on having Jeri speak at your company or conference, or on ordering bulk quantities of this book (customization available), please contact:

Driving Improved Results
610 5th Avenue #833
New York, NY 10185
212-923-5820
jeri@DrivingImprovedResults.com

Join Our Network of
International CEO Mastermind Groups
for Small/Midsize Businesses

The Concept: 12-20 owners of small and mid-size businesses from 2 countries come together for business opportunities and growth, leadership, and cross cultural exchange

Why: Because we grow when our assumptions are challenged by learning how others do things in different cultures, because business coaching/consulting drives improved results, because the world is getting smaller and we want to be an active player, because there are financial opportunities, because we want to grow personally and professionally, because understanding and communication generate peace making the world a better place for our children.

What's in it for each participant: 1) Individual and group coaching on business leadership, company culture development, business growth, customer loyalty, delegation, engaging employees, marketing, systems & processes, international trade, 2) Get taken out of your comfort zone by intimately understanding the culture and thought processes of a business person from another part of the world, 3) Be exposed to new sourcing, sales and collaboration opportunities as well as how to look for them, 4) Get exposed to speakers on topics of international finance and trade

What it looks like: 1) *Virtually-* monthly online group and individual sessions over the course of one year, 2) *In Person* – an annual trip to visit the CEO's in the other country and the opportunity to host the visiting CEO's in your own country

When: Groups now forming.

Seeking: Participants, facilitators, sponsors, board members, connections

Want to find out more? Contact Jeri Quinn, 212-923-5820, jeri@DrivingImprovedResults.com

Made in the USA
Charleston, SC
01 May 2014